Living Water,

Living Stories

To Nancy w. me deep
appreciation for your
wisdom.
Bebe

Living Water, Living Stories

African-American Women and Their Biblical Sisters

Bebe L. Baldwin

Alika Galloway, Editor

ISBN-10: 1502448262

ISBN-13: 978-1502448262

For the women who shared their stories as part of the living story of God's love and justice

Geraldine Anderson

Janet Beasley

Doris Benifield

Peggy Brewer

Ruby Brown

"Cassandra"

Jerry Dabney

Rita Dixon

Holley Dubose

Iesha Gillian

Virginia Howard

Regina Irwin

Deborah Isabelle

Beverly Larkin

Tammie Moore

Tara Parrish

Gloria Reese

Alanna Tyler

Arlene Walker

Caroline Wanga

Contents

Acknowledgments

There is no way I can express my deep respect and appreciation for the women who shared their stories with me. Their insights into the stories of the biblical sisters helped me to step inside the Scripture in ways I could never have imagined.

Each woman's story is precious and has enriched my own life beyond measure. The stories bear witness to the theme of this book, that the biblical story of God's love and justice continues today in the lives of people of faith.

Each woman who shared her story with me for this book has full license and permission to use, reproduce, and share her own story, because the content of the story is hers.

Every woman at Kwanzaa has a story to tell. I regret that it was impossible to include every woman's story in this book. Nevertheless, I would like to thank the many women at Kwanzaa whose faith, love, and acceptance have created a church family where stories can be shared.

Without the wise counsel of the Reverend Dr. Alika Galloway, this book would never have become a reality. She trusted me to write the stories of women she holds dear. She was my patient guide, picking me up when I stumbled and sharing her deep understanding of Scripture and the realities of women's lives.

I would also like to express my appreciation to the Reverend Dr. Rita Dixon who agreed not only to be interviewed but to write her reflections for the introduction in this book.

I am grateful to the members of the Kwanzaa Task Force of the Presbytery of the Twin Cities Area for their continuing advocacy and support for Kwanzaa's mission and to the church where I worship, Westminster Presbyterian Church in Minneapolis. Under the creative leadership of the Reverend Dr. Tim Hart-Anderson and the Reverend Doug Mitchell, the partnership between Kwanzaa and Westminster has enriched the lives of both congregations. This is the connectional church in action.

I give thanks to my adult children — Mike, Elizabeth, Carol, and Doug — for being my cheering section. Special thanks to artist Elizabeth whose creative talent produced the beautiful cover design.

Most of all, this book could never have been written or produced without the patience and love of my husband and best friend, Rollie Baldwin. After many years of marriage, we remain committed to each other and to God's dream of a world where all people can live with justice and peace.

Foreword

Stories As Living Water

The stories in this book embody love, fear, hope, anxiety, resiliency, trauma, and courage. These are true stories even if the facts may vary. The truth is not found in facts. It is found in the soul — in the wells of scattered remembrances, in the tears and the triumphs that are shared in this sacred text. These stories embrace the human condition and share sacred truths garnered through lived revelatory experiences.

The stories open the reader to experience the holy in new and magnificent ways. The holy whispers and weaves its mysterious presence throughout this work. Readers are invited, as they experience the fine nuances and bold proclamations, to marry their lives with the teller, with the narrative, with the tough truths and hard found lessons to become more human and, as such, more like the divine. These stories are living water, quenching the soul of its thirst for truth, meaning, purpose, and holy prophetic imagination.

These stories are leadership narratives. They are told in the hope that the teller inspires someone else to lead. As the ancient ones speak, they remind us that each of us has an ethical responsibility to teach what we have learned. My grandmother said it this way: "Each one must teach one." We each have the responsibility to take someone else on a spiritual journey, a journey of academic excellence, a journey out of the crack house, a journey out of despair and hopelessness to a place of revival, a place of spiritual rest, a journey of triumph, a journey of abundance.

These stories are living water. They provide a GPS to a land full of hope where the deep wells of holiness can be attained. The road of the journeys are never easy; they are fraught with potholes, but our sisters point the way. They send encouragement through the wind as they embody our collective consciousness and remind us, through soul power, that the way may be difficult, but all journeys start and end with the possibility of living water and abundant life.

Every sentence in this book is the reflection of two and perhaps three persons: Bebe Baldwin the listener, the ancient teller of the story, and the Kwanzaa sister whose story is told with honesty, clarity, love, and truth. These are humans created in the image of the divine. Our ancient ones share their stories mysteriously through the power of spirit connection. Their stories pierce the veils of silence that have subjugated them. The ancient ones, like the Kwanzaa women, full of divine presence, at times whispered their stories as a gift to God, as a silent thank you, as a holy dance in awe of "how they got over."

All the women, both the ancient sisters and the Kwanzaa sisters, shared their truths, revealed their testimony, and testified to the goodness of God because the Spirit, working and weaving its magic, told them that it was safe to do so as the Spirit opened Reverend Baldwin's ears to hear their heart in between the lines of hope and despair. These stories capture the heart, feed the soul, and nourish the body and mind with living water poured through sacred vessels.

These stories are sacred. They are living water for both the teller and those who will listen to them and, in doing so, find their own stories, remember their stories, and honor the listener through the telling. Stories are largely what enable us to communicate values and virtues such as love, courage, peace, and audaciousness. In the sharing of our stories, we come to grips with our realities and our choices … our defeats, defects, double mindedness, and our disillusionments. In the telling we find a sense of quiet grace and moral courage to do as our ancestors say, "Keep on keeping on."

Our stories unite us; they act as agents of human agency, solidarity, and strength. Stories are umbilical cords, cords that keep us tied to one another throughout the ages. These cords, though tattered, remind us that we are not on this journey alone and, through that remembrance, we are strengthened and encouraged to pass our wisdom along from generation to generation.

In *Living Water, Living Stories: African-American Women and Their Biblical Sisters*, women have provided text from their lives and have married them to the text of their ancestors. They baptized their words with their tears, and their tears erupted into a perpetual stream of life and light, hope, resilience, laughter, levity, and longing. This is the ancient way of life — the way of the story, of the narrative. It is the living canon of God's revelatory agency among God's people from one generation to the next. It is what we mean when we sing, "From everlasting to everlasting you are our God!"

In womanist ways it is one of the reasons we sing, "Take me to the water to be baptized." In the water we are baptized by ancient stories of our biblical ancestors and by new stories of our postmodern sisters. Together we are refreshed, renewed, and redeemed by living water. We hope that you will taste and see that the Lord is good as you drink from the well of water that never runs dry.

—*Reverend Dr. Alika Galloway*

Introduction

Reflections by the Reverend Bebe Baldwin

Sometimes an idea comes like a gentle whisper, tentative and uncertain. But that quiet moment can be a gift of grace. The idea for this book was born during a talk by the Reverend Dr. Alika Galloway at Westminster Presbyterian Church in Minneapolis.

Alika told stories of giftedness, of commitment, and of overcoming barriers as she spoke about the "bent-over" women at Kwanzaa Community Presbyterian Church. She related the stories to the Gospel narrative of Jesus' healing of the woman whose back had been bent for eighteen years (Luke 13:10–17). What I did not know was that I was about to begin a spiritual journey, one that would mark and shape me in ways I could never have imagined.

For some time before Alika's program, I had been working on a series of stories about women in the Bible, creating midrashim using research into the context of the texts and what I could discover about the culture of the time. I used my own insight, as a woman, into what I believed would have been the joys, fears, and hopes of the women as they faced the choices and challenges of their lives. I knew that entering fully into the lives of the women who lived thousands of years ago was impossible, given the chasm between the cultures of the ancient Middle East and twenty-first century America. The task was humbling.[1] Nevertheless, I believe that the stories are timeless and universal in ways that speak to us today. Bible study must be more than an academic pursuit; it must challenge and change us.

As I researched and reflected, I found myself drawn into the stories. It was as if the biblical women were inviting me to step into their lives. They became my friends and my sisters. The possibility of writing parallel stories of modern women began to beckon me.

As Alika spoke, an idea began to take shape. I knew that among the women at Kwanzaa there must be leaders such as Deborah, prophets such as Miriam, advocates such as the Syrophoenician woman. Could I, a white feminist process theologian, capture the gifts and the spirit of African-American women at Kwanzaa? Was this what God was calling me to do, to call the church to " ... hear the voices of peoples long silenced ... "?[2]

1

Alika and I had formed a rich friendship, so I believed that she would be honest with me. After the meeting I approached her with my idea. She agreed readily, but at the time I had no idea of what I was asking and how much she was risking, given her love and respect for the women and the long and tragic relationships between white and Black women.

Soon after our conversation, Alika issued an invitation to the women of Kwanzaa. She asked any who would consider being interviewed for a book to attend a meeting. When we gathered, she and I explained the project.

The question was, "Will African-American women trust a white woman with their stories?" Alika was watching and listening for their responses to me and to the proposal. Her affirmation, however, let them know that she trusted me — and so could they. Nearly all the women signed up for interview times. We asked each volunteer to choose a biblical woman in whose life she discovered her own story.

I began to interview the following week. That was the beginning — but only the beginning — of a long and intensive process. Our conversations continued — sometimes at the church, sometimes over coffee or lunch or dinner in my home. Sometimes there were tears; always there were hugs. We shared other experiences — worship, recipe exchanges, telephone conversations, and many follow-up interviews. Alika was my patient guide, picking me up when I stumbled, often explaining what I was hearing, and interpreting what I was missing between the lines. She knew the women so well that she was able to suggest directions our conversations might take.

I was amazed, often humbled, by how much I had to learn, at how much growing I needed to do. For many years I had been an advocate for social justice. During the Civil Rights Era, I had worked to promote understanding in white congregations. I had worked for school integration. Our youngest son was a voluntary participant in a desegregated city school.

When our family moved to Clearwater, Florida, we joined Church of the Reconciler, a multicultural congregation organized by the United Presbyterian Church to model reconciliation between the races. The church was located on a former lynching site. I was introduced to the Confession of 1967, with its call to a ministry of reconciliation. I began to understand — and I still believe — that "God's reconciling work in Jesus Christ and the mission of reconciliation ... are the heart of the gospel ... "[3]

During our years at Church of the Reconciler, I met many strong African-American women, more than I can name. Two who influenced me most deeply were Liz Simmons and Christine Morris. Liz was a mother to her family, to her neighborhood, and to the church. Christine and I taught church school together and developed curriculum for children based on liberation theology.

Sometime after our return to Minneapolis, the Presbytery of the Twin Cities Area took the bold step of working with the community in north Minneapolis to organize the first Afro-centric Presbyterian Church in Minnesota. The new congregation would be unique in that, from the very beginning, the worshipping, learning, serving community would merge with the church's mission in a neighborhood with high rates of poverty, unemployment, and crime. Alika and her husband, the Reverend Dr. Ralph Galloway, were called as co-pastors. My husband and I were both appointed to the Presbytery Steering Committee to help Kwanzaa connect to Presbytery resources. Soon after chartering, the Kwanzaa "family" grew to include representatives of several Presbyterian churches who formed a task force to interpret Kwanzaa's mission to Presbytery. It was the connectional church in action.

I felt accepted as part of the Kwanzaa family. Nevertheless, I had so much to learn! Alika tutored me in womanist theology as I listened and wrote and listened some more. The women shared stories of using their gifts in medicine, business, advocacy, and parenting in order to make a better world for their children and their communities. They trusted me with stories of new life that had risen out of despair. I heard stories of lived faith that is open to the Spirit, that does not lean upon pietistic platitudes but that comes out of daily experiences, the communal life of women who see in Jesus a model and companion for their lives.

I had immersed myself in the stories of biblical women. Yet in our conversations I discovered new and enriched meanings in the texts. I learned how a survivor of childhood sexual abuse discovered herself in the story of the woman at the well and could say, "Her story is my story." I learned how a talented, gifted young woman experienced, in the story of the hemorrhaging woman, her own reaching for a wider world. The women confirmed for me that the canon is alive and speaks to us today.

I learned of a healing community where people can tell their stories and be loved and accepted without being judged. I learned why the Black church has helped her people to survive, to overcome, to stand, to walk, to sit-in, to preach, to sometimes die for justice. I learned that the white church will never be whole until we confess that every time an African American was lynched, Jesus was there on the lynching tree.[4]

Each "modern" story in this book is a gift, a sacred gift to our readers. Each story bears witness to my conviction that the story of God's love and liberation did not end with our Scriptures. The canon is not closed; the stories continue in the lives of faithful women and men.

Each story invites readers to discover their own biblical sisters so that each one can say, "Her story is my story." And so the story that began with the biblical women is continuing with today's women of faith and will continue into the future.

My hope is that this book will help to build bridges of understanding between women who have been separated by our nation's tragic history, by race, and too often, by socioeconomic class. My prayer is that each story will be a witness to the reconciling work of Christ that transcends the boundaries we erect. Thanks be to God!

Reflections by Reverend Dr. Rita Dixon

When my dear friend, the Reverend Alika Galloway, first asked me to allow the Reverend Bebe Baldwin to interview me for a book they were creating, I reluctantly consented. However, I really thought she was out of her mind because I felt that there was nothing about my life that would be interesting enough for others to read. I was not even interested in remembering past experiences, much less reading about them.

How I dreaded the approaching interview with Bebe! But, at the very beginning of the first call, I recognized in her a kind and gentle spirit that immediately put me at ease. We shared a few experiences and laughs about our mutual friend, Alika, and I began to experience her as another loving friend. Her simple questions and gentle probing inspired me to share some of my previously long forgotten life experiences, some very painful.

By the end of the first interview, I was in a high spiritual state, felt very good about the process, and was amazed at how much was stored in my memory. Somehow the pain was transformed into joy through the sharing of it. I felt renewed, lighter, and happy to be me! Healing from some of the difficult experiences had occurred. I was actually amazed that I had lived through all those experiences.

When I read the first draft of my story, I was more than elated. What a gift! I was so grateful to see this creative story of some of my most significant life experiences on paper, words giving incarnation to memories that I had forgotten. It was an expression of me that would be shared with others. I felt deeply known and affirmed.

I was so inspired by the stories of women in the Bible and the women of Kwanzaa. The biblical characters were very familiar, but Bebe's presentation of their stories was new. I was seeing them through the lenses of scholarly research that provides information not given in Scripture and through insights from today's modern Western culture.

Bebe presents these biblical women who lived in ancient communities with a new perspective that didn't exist at the time these stories were written. She gives us another way to find meaning in biblical stories. She recreates her stories in light of today's evolving consciousness of human rights and justice for women, casting a new light on each character and her life situation.

Another area of reflection was provided by reading the stories of the Kwanzaa women. "What are stories? How can we find meaning in them? Who are we, and how can we see God working in and through us?"

As I read each of the stories, I recognized a piece of myself in every story. In many ways their stories expanded mine. Seeing them in print gave a stronger sense of meaning to my existence.

I hope this book will help all who read it recognize the importance of their own stories. Sharing our stories affirms our existence. It is a way of discerning God working in and through us. It is a source of healing. It makes visible our unity with the human family, even with our human families in the ancient communities of the Bible. We need one another to help us remember and see beyond our own cultural contexts.

And finally, may we all become more faithful in living in awareness of our connection to God, knowing that we are more than our experiences, more than our stories, that we are one in the Spirit, one in the God of the universe.

---

1. For an excellent analysis of the differences between first-century Palestine and American culture, see Richard L. Rohrbaugh, *The New Testament in Cross Cultural Perspective,* especially Chapter 1.

2. A Brief Statement of Faith — Presbyterian Church (U.S.A.), 70, *The Book of Confessions*. Louisville, KY: The Office of the General Assembly, 1999.
3. The Confession of 1967, 9.06. *The Book of Confessions*.
4. See James H. Cone, *The Cross and the Lynching Tree*.

Part I

As we step into these ancient stories, they inform our faith, shape our lives, and gift us with wisdom.

Living the Story: An Interview with the Reverend Dr. Alika Galloway and Cassandra's Story

S tories of our biblical ancestors speak to us across the centuries. As we step into those ancient stories, they inform our faith, shape our lives, and gift us with wisdom. They speak to us of oppression and liberation, of pain and joy, of death and new life. But God's revelation, the canon, is not closed. It continues to call us today through the diverse lives of women and men of faith.

Many conversations with the Reverend Dr. Alika Galloway have made this book possible. Her commitment to the living canon inspired, guided, and enlivened its writing. It is her conviction, and mine, that the canon speaks to us today, and that it can be discerned in the lives of the African American women whose stories are included in this collection.

When the Presbytery of the Twin Cities Area called Alika and her husband, the Reverend Dr. Ralph Galloway, to organize a new church in Minneapolis, the Presbytery's vision was radical. The Galloways were charged with starting a worshipping congregation and, at the same time, doing community engagement. "We were charged with doing both, but nobody knew how to do it. We were all shooting in the dark, trying to do God's will. I think sometimes that's when the best work is done. If you can see around the corner, you won't go," says Alika. In spite of the challenges, the new congregation and friends from Presbytery celebrated the chartering of Kwanzaa Community Presbyterian Church on February 24, 2002.

The Galloways created an unconventional strategy for organizing the new church. Alika had prepared for the academy; she had not expected to enter pastoral ministry, much less to organize a new church. Her "lack of preparation," however, had equipped her for a new vision for doing ministry. Her perspective, as a womanist and liberation theologian, told her that she had to find the women in the community and hear their stories. "Women tell, through their stories, how the community is doing," she says. She sought out women in the neighborhood, sat on their front steps, and listened. She didn't tell

8

them that she was organizing a new church, but, "I think they figured it out. They were just glad to have someone listen to their stories."

Sitting on front porches, Alika began to hear the heartbeat of the community through the women's stories. They spoke of husbands and sons who had lost their sense of self-worth through long periods of unemployment. She heard of young men dealing drugs with customers who drove in from affluent communities and of young girls trading sex for a good meal or a place to sleep. She learned of parents who worked two or three jobs to support families but often had to choose between buying groceries and keeping the lights on. She listened to parents' fears for their children's safety.

She heard stories of remarkable strength and resilience. She met neighbors who reached out to one another and gave support in times of crisis. She talked with single moms who, along with working and caring for children, were earning GEDs or college degrees. She discovered women whose deep faith had sustained them, who lived the life of the spirit that affirms and liberates.

Looking back, she reflects, "I was not prepared for traditional ministry, but I was given a great perspective for listening and knowing the value and legitimacy of stories. This is the African way. The truth is in the lives of the people."

The tradition of sharing stories continues at Kwanzaa. "Ralph and I tell our stories," Alika says. "That gives other people permission to tell their stories and see God's revelatory agency in their stories. This makes the Bible a living hermeneutic.

"From listening to stories, we dissect the issues, strengths, barriers, struggles, and challenges. Within the story is the lived canon. That is why this book is so important.

"Within the story we can ask, 'How is God's revelatory purpose manifested in our lives and how do we know it? Can you see yourself in the biblical story? Can you see yourself excluded, exiled outside the camp like Miriam? Can you see yourself as Mary, a teenage mom being blamed by the community?' When you see yourself in the story, you recognize God's revelatory agency but also discover God's continuing love and purpose for you. As oppressed people, you no longer see yourselves as having no worth. You know, 'I'm in the Bible!' "

When I ask Alika how Kwanzaa carries on the tradition of storytelling, she says, "You set yourself down. You listen as people tell their stories. You listen without judging. This is deep listening, engaging in critical conversations. But to do this, you have to create safe places for confidentiality and competency. That's what it means to be family; we tell our stories."

As they share and listen to their stories, members of Kwanzaa are cherishing and nurturing relationships. This is what Alika calls the "prime value" for the church family. "We don't live independently; we are interdependent," she says. "That's why we have dual leadership at Kwanzaa. Ralph and I are like the yin and the yang.

"There is no competition at Kwanzaa, no hierarchy. We are all God's beloved. The community helps people process their gifts and puts them to work. Our mission is, 'Go get them, bring them in, grow them up, send them out.'

"But we are not looking for perfection. We're looking for purpose. Perfection is God's job. Ours is to open the door."

Reflecting on the years at Kwanzaa, Alika says, "I am not qualified to be a pastor, but God's presence has been so real and I'm grateful. Kwanzaa has been the gift to me. I hope other people have been blessed, but it's been my gift, my place of salvation."

But the gifts of Kwanzaa do not stop with Alika. The women who shared their stories have offered their gifts to the readers of this book. In Alika's words, "The women's ancestral teaching continues, and that gives wisdom. As women we combine this wisdom and go tell somebody."

This is wisdom that is shared, sometimes on front porches, sometimes in kitchens, sometimes in the safety of the church family. This is the canon that lives and testifies to the Presence in today's world of our God who is all-loving and all-wise.

Cassandra's Story: From Front Porch to New Life

Cassandra's new life began its birthing as she and Pastor Alika talked, sitting on the front steps of a house across a driveway from the church. Many months had to pass, however, before she found the courage to walk across the driveway and step inside the church.[1] It was Easter Sunday, the celebration of new life.

"Alleluias" swelled to greet the Day of Resurrection as Pastor Ralph's voice rose in a rich crescendo to proclaim, "He is risen! He is risen!" Worshippers clapped, swayed, and flung arms high in praise. Even the light that streamed through stained glass danced and the walls seemed about to burst with the joy of the morning.

Far back in the sanctuary, Cassandra was asking herself, "Do I belong here?" Her head was bowed, and one hand gripped a thick roll of paper. Hidden in the roll was a painting, a secret gift, meant to be seen only by the pastors.

Cassandra discovered — or was discovered by — Kwanzaa when she lived next door to the church in a house used by drug hustlers. Pastor Alika often sat on Cassandra's front steps and talked. She invited her to Kwanzaa, but Cassandra could not yet see a way beyond her life.

She watched people going and coming from Kwanzaa but could not envision herself in church, sitting beside those "good people." She was sure she would be "out of place" and would never be accepted. Many months passed before she could take that risk.

The turning point arrived. On a night before Easter, she felt herself being pulled toward the church. She stayed up all night painting. Later she said of her creation, "It wasn't my best work, but it meant something to me."

When morning came, she ventured across the lawn and the parking area that separated her house from the church. She carried the precious painting she planned to share with the pastors. She found a seat in the back of the church.

Pastor Alika, however, did not let Cassandra escape unnoticed. Toward the end of the service she called from the front of the sanctuary, "Come on up, Cassandra. What's that you've got?"

Cassandra could no longer hide herself or her painting. She walked to the front of the sanctuary, hesitated, and then unrolled the work of her private Easter vigil.

Pastor Alika removed the pulpit hanging and, in its place, hung Cassandra's painting. Jesus, as tall as the pulpit, looked out into the congregation. In his arms he held two lambs, one black and one white. Cassandra says, "I felt accepted!" Her new life began that Easter morning.

1. I have changed the name of the woman in this story. I have used the real names in all the other stories.

Redeeming the Story: A Letter to the Church from Mary Magdalene, Mark 16:1–13

I was first at the empty tomb, the first witness to the resurrection. Why did you defame my name? Why did you call me a prostitute?

I was Jesus' faithful disciple. Jesus wasn't like other men. He honored and respected women. He even listened to us. Once he changed his mind after a woman argued with him! (Mark 7:24–30)

As for myself, I drank in every word he spoke, thirsty for that living water. As he shared food with the hungry, as he healed the sick in body and the heavy in heart, I knew the presence of God. It gave me and the other women joy to help bring in God's reign by supporting Jesus and his followers from our own wealth.

When Jesus was arrested, the men ran away. Perhaps their dreams of an all-powerful Messiah were shattered. Perhaps only vulnerable women could imagine a Messiah who did not wield military power.

So we were the ones who watched and waited. When Jesus was beaten, we felt the lashes. When he hung on the cross, we wept with pain. When the sword pierced his side, it pierced our hearts. When he died, something inside us died too.

There was one more thing we must do — wrap Jesus' body in precious spices. Protected by the darkness early in the morning after the sabbath, we hurried to the tomb. We worried about not being able to roll away the heavy stone. It was as though by clinging to that one thought we could hold back our pain.

When the darkness parted with the dawning of first light, the tomb rose before us. But instead of the stone, the entrance gaped. Had we been granted a small miracle, or had our minds been clouded by grief?

We rushed in. Then we stopped, stunned. We looked in disbelief at the place where Jesus' body had lain.

Was some cruel demon toying with our grief? I wanted to scream at heaven, "Can't I have this single bit of comfort? Doesn't my Lord deserve this last bit of respect?"

Shock ... anger ... then terror gripped me. If Pilot was so afraid of a Galilean rabbi that he had Jesus' body stolen, what would the Romans do next? Would they unleash their cruel power on Jesus' followers?

Then we saw him—a man robed in white. "Do not be alarmed," he said, "you are looking for Jesus of Nazareth, who was crucified. He has been raised; he is not here ... But go, tell his disciples and Peter that he is going ahead of you to Galilee; there you will see him, just as he told you."

I could not take in his words. I fled from the tomb. When I was able to gasp out the news, no one believed me. Who, besides Jesus, would believe the word of a woman?

So why did you call me a sinful woman? Why did you change my story? I was not the penitent woman Luke wrote about — the one Jesus used to teach Simon a lesson on forgiveness. I was not the adulterous woman Jesus saved from stoning. I was not even Mary of Bethany, even though she too was a follower of Jesus. Later churchmen combined our stories.

After the resurrection, your gospels dropped my story. Paul did not name me as a witness to the resurrection. (I Corinthians 15:5) But gospels that are not in your Bible speak of me. One calls me Jesus' "companion."[1] One says that I always walked with Jesus. Another says that when the disciples, including Peter, were confused and dejected after the resurrection, I was the one who reminded them of Jesus' teaching and urged them to be faithful.[2] Because I am a woman, I was not counted among the apostles, but some early Christians called me the "apostle to the apostles."

You may have heard some of the legends about me. Some say that I spent thirty years in a cave doing penance for my sins. Would a loving God require that? If God does require that kind of penance, what of the men who ran away — especially the one who denied Jesus three times?

Saint Augustine turned me into a temptress. I became the voluptuous woman whose sin titillated "holy" men. Homes founded for the "salvation" of "fallen" girls and women were named for me. Maybe they should have been named for the men who violated them.

Why did you change my story? Were you so in need of a symbol of repentance? Or did you associate me with sin because the Gospel says that Jesus drove out seven demons? If you knew the New Testament, you would know that demon possession meant illness, not sin. But some church people still associate illness and disability with sin. Even in your modern "enlightened" age, you have probably heard someone say, "His illness/disability is God's punishment for his sins!"

But I am writing to you not only for myself but for my sisters — the Mary Magdalenes of your day. Are you letting them tell you their own stories or have their stories been stolen from them?

My sisters still feel the pain of the innocent. Some are working for peace. Some are working to end poverty. Some are working to end abuse or oppression or ignorance. They are bringing their own gifts — the most precious being their lives.

Some of my sisters are labeled "radical," "mad," "obsessed." Yet they continue to take their own kind of spices to the tombs where injustice has tried to destroy hope. They too have a message of new life. Pray for them; they are my sisters — and yours.

If you will listen to me, the Mary of the gospels and of the earliest Christian tradition, I can teach you so much. I was close to Jesus. I can teach you about listening, about faithfulness, about discipleship.

Then, like me, you will discover the empty tomb where hope triumphs over despair. Like me, you will tremble for it is not an easy discovery. You may wish to run away. You may tell your story to those who do not want to hear. But even then, you will know the Presence of the Living Christ — always and eternally with us.

1. This quote is from the Gospel of Philip, written in the second half of the third century CE. The book is not included in our New Testament. The quote is cited by Susan Haskin in *Mary Magdalene: Myth and Metaphor*. Old Saybrook, Conn.: Konecky and Konecky, 1993, p. 29.
2. This story is told in the *Gospel of Mary Magdalene*. Rochester, Vt.: Inner Traditions, 2002, p. 9. This gospel is not included in our New Testament. It dates from the third century CE and was discovered in Egypt in 1945.

Part II

The truth is in the lives of the people.
—Alika Galloway

CHAPTER 1

Living Beauty: Hagar and Tara

Hagar's Story, Genesis 21:8–19

We are walking to freedom, my son and I. Our lives have been spared. We are no longer a slave woman and a castaway son. We are free!

I was not born a slave. My father was the king of Egypt, but what was I to him? My mother was but one of his many wives.

When I was a young girl, I was thought to be very beautiful. My mother called me Precious Jewel because she said my eyes flashed like two gems in a setting of gold, the color of my skin. She loved to stroke my cheeks because she said they were as smooth and soft as a newborn's. Now they are blistered and burned, as rough as the blowing sands that seep through the heavy veils we wear to protect ourselves from the desert wind.

My mother tried to arrange a good marriage for me. She petitioned my father to give me to a prince from one of the royal houses. But I think he judged me too high-spirited for court life because he used me as a peace offering to a tough old desert warrior. Abraham is a landless chief who leads his clan and flocks from oasis to oasis, always on the move. His camp smells like goats.

Sarah and Abraham's people have a saying that welcoming a stranger is more important than welcoming their God. I was a stranger in their clan, but there was no welcome for me. Abraham's kin and the other servants taunted me for my dark skin that was thought so beautiful in Egypt. They laughed at my first attempts to grind the barley for the flat, heavy cakes they eat. I had to struggle to force down the food they live on. (Oh, if only I could taste again the fine wheat bread, the dates and honey and pomegranates we ate every day in Egypt!)

I'll admit that I never treated my mistress with much respect, especially after I got pregnant. Life is hard in this cruel land, and families need many children to do the work. If a wife cannot conceive, everyone knows that her God is displeased and has denied her children. No wonder Sarah raged when her bleeding came with every new moon. Sometimes a black cloud wrapped her in sullen silence, and I could do nothing to please her. Sometimes I tried to hate her, but whenever I touched the edge of my own anger, I remembered that both she and I were caught like insects in a web that neither of us could escape. Our women's bodies decree our fate; our destiny is to bear children, especially sons. In that way she and I were sisters. Even Sarah, with the authority that she held in the family, could not escape her role as breeder. She was renowned for her beauty, but the God who had given her perfection of face and body had not granted her a single child.

Then one night Sarah approached me, desperation burning in her eyes. Her voice, as she gave her command, was shrill, as if she needed to push away her own feelings or any hesitation she felt. "Go to my husband's tent. You will bear his heir."

I stood, unable to move. I was stunned. I was sure I had misunderstood.

"Why are you standing there? Stupid girl! Go!" I obeyed my mistress.

When my belly began to swell, I swung it forward every chance I had, pointing it, flaunting it at Sarah. Sometimes she looked at me as if she wanted to strike me, but I reminded her, every chance I had, that I was carrying a big healthy baby, her husband's heir.

But a day came when I could take no more. My mistress's face was so dark, her voice so shrill that I feared for my life and for the life of my unborn child. I ran away. I had no idea where I was going. I simply fled into the merciless desert.

My bitter freedom didn't last long. I was filling my water skin at a spring when a man appeared. I was terrified; I dropped my water, spilling the most precious gift of the desert.

"Where have you come from? Where are you going?" asked the man.

"I'm running away from my mistress."

"Go back and obey her!" he commanded.

"Go back? Obey?" Only a messenger from Abraham would demand that, I thought. I opened my mouth to object as I glanced around to seek a way to escape.

But before I could move, he went on. "God knows what you have suffered. You will have a son and call him Ishmael. I will multiply your descendants."

I threw myself at the messenger's feet. I tried to speak but I was shaking so hard that I could not control my voice. I could barely stammer, "You are God, and I have seen you!" Abraham's people say that to see God is to die, but I have seen God and I am alive!

When my shaking had calmed enough so that I could stand, I grabbed my waterskin. I ran. My body had lost its grace. I felt heavy and clumsy, but my heart was light. I knew that no matter what I had to face when I returned, God had spoken to me, a woman. God had made a promise to me, a slave!

My time came and I delivered my son. As I labored, Sarah crouched behind me as if she, not I, was giving birth. But I, not Sarah, gave Abraham his first son.

After that I took every chance to put on airs. Whenever I spoke of Ishmael, I made sure that I said, "My son, Ishmael." When I called him, I shouted out so everyone could hear, "Ishmael, my son, my son!" You may think that I was using my son only to taunt Sarah, but that was not the way it was. I marveled at every movement of his beautiful little body. I heard music in every baby word that he spoke. I adored my son.

Ishmael's birthright didn't last long. After many years of barrenness, Sarah amazed herself and everyone else by bearing her own son. She named him Isaac, which means "laughter," because both she and Abraham had laughed at the very idea that they could have a child when Sarah was ninety and Abraham was one hundred years old. Laughter was as plentiful as food and drink at the feast Abraham gave on the day Isaac was weaned. I twisted my lips into a smile, but my heart could not laugh. I feared for my son.

From that day on I felt as though the ground I walked on was rumbling. It was as if an earthquake was gathering its strength to split my world apart. Behind the mask that hid Sarah's true feelings, I sensed a simmering rage.

So I was not surprised when my worst fears became real. Early one morning as the first rays of sunlight were reaching for our camp, I woke to see Abraham leaning over me. He was holding out one loaf of bread and a single waterskin. Before he opened his mouth to tell me to take my son and go, I knew.

But where could we go? There was no place but the cruel desert. In the gathering light of early dawn, I saw a single tear glistening on the leathered skin of the old patriarch, but he could not allow himself to take one last look at the son he was throwing away. A loaf of bread and a skin of water — how long would they last? Abraham had treated strangers who wandered into the camp with more generosity.

So we walked alone into the desert, my son and I. No one ventured into the merciless wilderness without caravan or clan, but there we were, a woman and a child. What was I to do — sell myself and my child to a passing caravan of traders? Should I pledge my labor and my body to another chief in payment for our lives? I thought it might be better to die.

I looked at our meager provisions. I tried to figure how much bread and how much water we could use each day to make them last as long as possible. Then I thought, "What difference does it make if we use it now or days from now? In either case we shall die."

My anger flared toward Abraham, the father who should have protected his son, and toward Sarah who, I was sure, had instigated our exile. I wanted to curse whatever god had sent me back to Sarah with the promise that I would be the mother of a great nation. "That god must be laughing at me now," I thought, "for being so easily fooled."

When we had squeezed the last drops of precious liquid from the waterskin and sifted the soil beneath our feet for any lost crumbs of bread, I laid my child under a bush. He wailed, too weak for a healthy scream. I crept away. I could not bear to listen to his crying or watch him die. I, who had fed him at my breast, had nothing to give him.

"Hagar!" Someone called my name. If I had had the strength, I would have screamed. Was it the voice of a demon? Was my pain a plaything for the gods?

Then I heard the words clearly: "God has heard the voice of the boy. Get up! Take him by the hand. Hold him! I will make him a great nation!" Again, I heard the promise. I shook my fist at the heavens, sure that some malicious god was playing a cruel joke on us.

Then I saw it — water — sparkling at my feet. I ran to Ishmael and swept him into my embrace. I carried him to the water. We drank until we could drink no more. I laughed until tears of sheer joy clouded my eyes. Holding my son, I danced in the overflow, splashing water over the thirsty ground.

So the God who gives life to the desert has given us this gift of new life. My child and I are walking now, hand in hand. Where are we going? I don't know yet but I trust in the new life we have been offered, the new life, the gift of God.

Tara's Story

Tara lay awake, sleepless, for three nights after she met Hagar in a seminary class. Like Hagar, Tara is a single mother. Like Hagar, Tara is a member of an oppressed group. Like Hagar, she discovered that God is faithful, that she and her child are loved by God.

Pregnancy changed the lives of both Tara and Hagar. Tara describes herself as having very low self-esteem before she got pregnant. As a pregnant thirty-year-old single woman, she had to face the negative feelings and accusations of other people. Nevertheless, she says of her pregnancy, "It made me feel powerful … having that life inside me." She recalls hearing other women complain about feeling ugly when they were pregnant. For Tara it was different: "I was full of life itself. It was awesome!"

Seeing her daughter, Makeda, for the first time was a transforming experience. "When I saw her, I thought I was the most powerful being there was. I thought, 'If I can do this by accident, what can I do on purpose?' It made me see all the possibilities. Wow!" She knew that she would never again have low self-esteem. "I looked at her and I saw beauty. I could see myself in her." Tara, who remembers being called "ugly" and "stupid" as a child, said, "I looked at my child and thought, 'How can I dislike me when she is so beautiful?' "

Tara's life as a single parent has not been easy. "The hardest thing is being a mother," she says. She's had to make hard choices, like always telling employers that her child comes first, that she has no parents or siblings or grandparents who can take over if Makeda gets sick. Tara knows that other people may disagree with some of her choices, but she says, "I have to listen to God." Referring again to Hagar's story, Tara says that just as Hagar ran away but then returned to Sarah and Abraham, "There have been times when I've wanted to run, but God said, 'Go back!' "

When she is asked what her biggest challenge is, Tara doesn't hesitate. "Balance!" She adds, "I have to make hard decisions so that I can keep all the balls in the air." As a single mother, employee, and seminary student, she often feels that she needs to "do everything." But she says, "Nothing can give when it comes to my daughter."

Balancing the many demands on her time and energy is a continuing struggle. She recalls a time when she was assigned to take over the responsibilities of a woman who was going on maternity leave.

The woman left her position early, before Tara had had time to learn her new tasks. She says that she became "unglued." She needed time alone, so she sacrificed several hours of pay to go home for what she calls "a personal retreat." "There comes a point when I have to take care of myself." At such times her prayer is for "some peace." She explains this by saying, "I can't be 'crazy.' Makeda has a privileged life, but she'll have a hard life if I'm 'crazy.' "

Tara's journey toward ministry began during her childhood. "Even as a small child I knew God had something great for me." She remembers going to church as a child and having fun with friends, but she says, "The Spirit wasn't there. We didn't know why we were going."

She became engaged to a man who she didn't realize was a drug addict. "I thought I could help him." She was in a relationship for three years and describes herself as being "desperately codependent."

One day Tara ran into an old friend. Seeing her distress, he asked, "What is going on?" This question forced Tara to face what was happening in her life. She says, "I was broken."

Hoping that God could help her, she began going to church again. Her pastor said something that changed her life. He said, "You are a child of God!" After being told, as a child, that she was "unlovable," that promise was like a spring bubbling up in the desert, like the very water of life.

Reflecting now on her new awareness, Tara asks herself, "What decisions would I have made if I had known God really loved me?" One decision she was able to make was to end her engagement even though she was in the process of planning her wedding.

When she is asked about her decision to attend seminary, Tara's first response is, "Pastor Alika hoodwinked me!" On a more serious note she went on to talk about school and career. She started college right after high school but was not challenged by her classes. She dropped out and held various jobs. She was working as a receptionist when a coworker stopped by her desk and told her emphatically that she should go back to college. Shortly after that, she returned to college and earned a BA in English literature from Metropolitan State University in Minneapolis. Since graduation she has worked in communications as a writer, English teacher, journalist, and corporate communicator. She did not find her work satisfying.

Still struggling to find her real vocation, she had a conversation with God. She says that God asked whether she was finally ready to listen. Her response was, "So you want me to go to seminary?" Finally after resisting for a long time, she enrolled at United Theological Seminary in New Brighton, Minnesota. She describes her decision as "the most right thing I have ever done." Tara reflects on her decision by thinking of the many women at Kwanzaa who have never had the opportunity for that kind of education:. "It is my privilege. How dare I waste that potential?"

But the balancing act continues. She admits that it's not easy, but says, "If I have to get up at three o'clock in the morning to balance everything, I'll do it!" The prayer of her Kwanzaa family is that Tara, like Hagar, will be able to "move through her situation, grow, and be blessed.

Questions for Reflection and Discussion

- What parallels do you find between the stories of Hagar and Tara?
- When did grace break into the life of each woman?
- Tell about a time when unexpected grace broke into your life.

For Further Exploration

- How has the story of Sarah and Hagar been repeated in the history of this country?
- Is the story continuing today? If so, in what way?
- What will it take to change the story?

CHAPTER 2

Living Hope: Puah and Arlene

Puah's Story, Exodus 1:15–21

The woman who answered the door looked at me as if I were a stranger, not Puah, the respected midwife. Lines of sour suspicion furrowed her wrinkled face. Without speaking, she stepped aside to let me in. The room stank of fear.

Confused, I wondered whether I was in the right house. A scream I recognized as the pain of a woman in labor told me that, yes, I was in the house of Milnah. Her time had come, and I had been summoned. But where was the welcome, the sense of relief that always greeted the midwife? The heat of too many bodies filled the room. Why had so many women joined Milnah's sisters to assist in the birth?

The women parted to let me pass through and examine my patient. Trying to hide my growing alarm, I looked into Milnah's eyes, but they were not taking in this world. What she saw was the face of death, already lurking in the room, waiting to snatch and carry her into the darkness.

Anger seized me. How long had she been in labor? Why had I not been called earlier? I gripped her hand and promised her, feigning the conviction I could not feel, that all would be well for her and for her baby. For a fleeting moment her eyes met mine, and I saw a glimmer of hope before she surrendered again to the threatening shadows.

I snapped orders to the women to carry my birthing stool and herbs into the house while I examined Milnah. As I was determining the progress of her labor, I urged her to return to the land of the living. I cooed; I comforted. With relief I discovered that in spite of her long hard labor, all would indeed be well if she could find the strength to deliver her child. I reassured her that soon she would be holding a big, healthy baby.

Suddenly I realized that the women had formed a protective wall around Milnah and me. All my senses were alert to Milnah's progress, but I stole quick glances at the women who surrounded us. There was Michal, whose six healthy babies I had delivered. There was Achah, whose first son I had saved by turning him so that his head was in the birthing position. There was Leah, whose nearly strangled infant I had breathed into life as I unwound the cord from around her neck. I knew all of them — women who had been delivered by my mother and whose mothers had been delivered by my grandmother. Their faces bore concern and compassion for Milnah, but I didn't understand why their faces were closed to me.

Milnah's pains were coming very close together. I rubbed her back and urged her on. As if they were taking her pain into their own bodies, the encircling women began to roll their own bellies. They chanted and sang birthing songs, "Be strong, mother; be strong." The room became like one womb writhing to give birth. And always, the circle tightened, closed in upon us, becoming smaller and smaller. My chest grew heavy. I feared I could not breathe, would choke if the circle came any closer.

Suddenly, the truth struck me. I knew. I knew why the distrust in the room was like the taste of sour wine.

Our houses have keen ears and sharp eyes. The news had already spread that the soldiers had come to my house with the king's order that the midwives must kill every son born to a Hebrew woman. The women in the circle — my neighbors and my friends — were afraid. They did not know whether I had come as their healer or as their enemy. I knew that they would not have called me if they had not feared for Milnah's life. They needed me but had come to protect Milnah's child.

A scream tore through the women's chanting. With one last torturous push, the baby's head, topped with dark hair over a red wrinkled face, appeared. Working with the skill of many years' experience, I caught the slippery body of a perfect male child.

The women were so close that I could feel their hot breath on my neck. The circle had tightened into a knot around me. I didn't need to look around me to know that the women were ready to spring, to strike, to protect the child if I made any unexpected move.

The silence in the room screamed. Even the baby's first cry did not signal the joyous singing that always congratulates the mother and welcomes the child. It was as if the house itself was holding its breath.

In my mind's eye, I saw the king. He was as real as if he had been in the room. He towered above me, resplendent in royal robes, wearing the jeweled crown and wielding the golden scepter that marked him as the child of the sun god. But I knew at that moment that he was not my God. My loyalty was to the God of my ancestors and to my people. The women in the room and their children were my people. Milnah's baby would live as would all the others I would deliver. I placed the infant at his mother's breast.

The women moved to embrace me as they began to sing of life, of hope, of joy. They sang and danced until loud pounding and commanding voices broke into our celebration.

I had no doubt; the king's soldiers had come, searching for a newborn and the midwife. As I stepped toward the door, I was sick at heart. I looked back to the mat where the infant had been nursing. All had changed. There was no evidence of a birth. Mother and child had disappeared. I knew then that as the other women and I had been singing and rejoicing, they had slipped silently away, as if vanishing into the safety of a silent night. The women had planned well. I gave thanks to the God of our deliverance.

But I knew I must go with the king's men, who would take me to the royal court. When I was accused, I would claim before the king, who was sitting on the throne of Egypt, that the Hebrew women were so strong that they delivered without the help of my skills as a midwife.

I have made my choice. I will stand with my people. I will be faithful to our God.

Arlene's Story

When the Masai people of Africa meet, they greet one another by asking, "How are the children?" In the neighborhood surrounding Kwanzaa Church, the correct answer for many families would be, "Not well."

No king has ordered the babies destroyed; no soldiers are waiting to arrest midwives. But the threats to the health, safety, and spirit of the children are as real as the violence waged by the pharaoh many years ago in Egypt. Gangs, drugs, and the sex trade offer "hope" to youth who are hungry or homeless, to those who are victims of street violence, to those who know little real hope for the future.

Arlene, a modern "midwife," has committed herself to helping families discover the hope that transforms lives. Her work is based in her faith, a faith shaped by her own struggles and her own despair. "A perfect match" is the way Arlene describes her life and the story of the midwife. "The babies are my focus," she says. "My focus is to save the babies, but I've got to get to the mothers first."

As a child Arlene dreamed of growing up to be a teacher. Her family's apartment was in a project in East St. Louis. Her parents and seven children shared one bathroom. That bathroom became Arlene's "classroom."

When class was in session, she locked herself in the bathroom and used her mother's soap to write on the metal door. When her mother called that she had been in there long enough, Arlene rubbed the soap off the door and her class was dismissed!

When Arlene was ten, her father died by drowning. This event, which Arlene calls a "starting point," changed and reshaped her life. She lost her childhood. "I never saw my life taking the turn it did," she says.

For many years she had a recurring dream about her father. He was leading the family over a bridge into a body of water. Then, just before they were all about to drown, she would awake.

The dream would end, but not Arlene's new reality. Her mother was left to raise seven children on her own. Her father had been the head of the household and paid all the bills. Her mother had had her first baby at fifteen and had dropped out of school. (Later, she earned her GED.) Arlene remembers her mother crying because she didn't know how to open a bank account.

Describing her relationship with her siblings during those years, Arlene says, "We were very close. We became our own parents. We had to make sure our mother was alright." When Arlene became a mother, she didn't know how to parent. Her mother tried to help, but Arlene says she was so angry that she shut her mother out of her life.

Anger because of her father's death drove Arlene for many years. "I got angry. I stayed angry for a long time." She blamed everyone for the direction her life was taking. "I was angry with the world — the system, the Black man, the white man, my mom, my dad, sisters, brothers, and God. Anger caused me to self-destruct. I started using drugs and dating men. It was very self-defeating behavior."

After she became the mother of three children, Arlene left East St. Louis and moved to Minneapolis. She was seeking a better environment for her family. She became so homesick, however, that she took a bus back to Illinois. Her stay there didn't last long. She turned around and boarded the first bus back to Minnesota.

In Minneapolis she continued to use drugs and alcohol. Working as a cashier, she was able to buy a house. She was proud of her fixer-upper. But she lost her home to drugs. Her son was taken out of her care and placed in protective custody. She was separated from her other two children. She says they were angry and "didn't want to bother with me."

Years passed before Arlene made any changes in her life. She recalls lying awake one night: "I realized that everything in my life was down the drain. I took a real good look at my life. I said, 'This ain't living.' " She knew that her life had gone wrong and that she had to find out how to change it.

She found a counselor who challenged her. Arlene describes her as "a very spiritual lady." She remembers the counselor saying, "I want you to come in here with an open mind." Arlene insisted that she had an open mind, but the counselor repeated, "Arlene, just have an open mind."

Arlene credits the counselor with helping her to understand what was happening in her life and why she had made the choices that she had. "Her words soothed me, and I surrendered. I held on to her for dear life."

Arlene continues, "The first thing was forgiveness. That was what really broke the ice. It wasn't until I was forty — I'm fifty-one now — that I was able to forgive God for the death of my father. Once I was able to let go and forgive God, my healing began."

Arlene found a healing community at Kwanzaa. She discovered Kwanzaa after a weeklong high. "I just got tired," she says.

On Saturday night when Arlene was getting ready for bed, "something" told her, "Get ready." That something wouldn't let her go. So before the sun came up the next morning, she was prepared — showered, dressed, and ready with her Bible. "I knew I was going to church."

It was a hot July morning. Arlene remembers walking many blocks along a busy main street in "a dazed state." She passed several other churches before she came to a corner where "something" directed her, "Turn here. Come on down the street." On the very next corner stood a brick church with the sign, Kwanzaa Community Church. She stumbled inside.

The woman who greeted her at the front door was no stranger. The two women had often talked on the bus when Arlene was on her way to the liquor store. The woman had talked to Arlene about Kwanzaa.

Arlene says about her first encounter with Kwanzaa, "I knew. I knew that this was where I was supposed to be. From that time on, I've been here. That's my life."

Arlene has been at Kwanzaa for eight years, "as long as I've been sober." She describes Kwanzaa as her family: "I have not met a group of people I love so dearly. They became my family — mother, father, aunties, uncles, brothers, and sisters. Everyone here has been that for me. I wouldn't trade it for the world. I tell everybody, 'If you've got a problem, come to Kwanzaa.' " Arlene says that when her daughter was struggling with addiction, "My family walked with me and prayed for my child."

As a vision for the future began to take shape, Arlene started college. She dreamed of opening a housing facility in collaboration with a treatment center. There, mothers struggling with addiction could live with their children while they received the support they needed as they moved toward healing. Her goal was very different from her childhood dream of teaching school, but it was one that was born out of her own experience.

Her studies were interrupted for a year while she cared for her daughter's children. She says she wanted to give them the stability they had never had. "I didn't want my grandchildren in the system. I didn't want them to be mistreated." Arlene says that being with her grandchildren and seeing their lives become stable gave her a "sense of well-being." Her daughter was able, eventually, to again care for her children.

Arlene returned to college and earned an associate degree in chemical dependency. At the time of this interview, she needed only two more courses to complete her Bachelor of Science. "I may go back and do something in human services."

Arlene is now case manager and therapist for African American Family Services. Her commitment is "restoring women back to life." She is convinced that this is the only way to save the children. "One of the things I think is such a blessing in the position God has put me in is that I've been through it myself. There is no judgment." She can relate to women's lack of self-esteem because she too has faced racism and been called "ugly."

Arlene says, "I tell the women, 'We're going to work through this. I'm going to get you the resources you need. We are going to work together to get you balanced — mind, body, spirit — so you can move forward in life.' "

Arlene admits that she has had much to learn. "I used to be the savior," she says. "Then, the Spirit told me, 'It is not for you to do the saving. All you do is plant the seed. I will water it and grow it up. I am

God and God alone. I don't need you to be God with me.' " To this Arlene could only answer, "Okay, I get it!"

At times her work seems overwhelming. She struggles to find balance in her life and work. She has had to learn that if she isn't getting the rest she needs, she cannot be effective. Therapy helped her learn to let go. "As I am driving home, I let the windows down. I say, 'That's gone! I'm not going to take it with me.' "

In her work Arlene is able to draw upon both her formal education and her personal experience. "When we're using, we live inside a box." One of her goals is to get women to reach out. "Inside the box there are only people who are doing what we do — drugs and alcohol. There is chaos and confusion." She says that as a result, the women and their children often end up in the system, dealing with the police and child protection. "That may be all the women have known. I tell the women, 'We're going to step outside the box.' "

She describes activities that help women to stretch their minds and lives. Recently they visited the Science Museum of Minnesota for an exhibit on the Dead Sea Scrolls. Another experience she describes as "awesome" was their participation at Day on the Hill, an annual event when people of diverse religious groups gather at the state capitol in St. Paul. "We had a wonderful day. The women got to talk with their legislators!" Meeting and expressing their concerns with community and state leaders was a giant leap for the women who had been held captive in boxes created by racism, poverty, and substance abuse. "I can talk at them all day long, but it's not the same. I tell them, 'Let me show you what it's like to be out in the community, to be outside the box.' "

For many years Arlene was trapped in her own box of self-destructive behavior. Now she guides others as they reach for hope and freedom. For many years she was driven by anger. Now she knows the grace of being able to forgive. Her own life experience has given her the gift of being able to relate and be trusted by mothers as she works with them to save their children.

Reflecting on the years when she was held captive by drugs and anger she says, "One thing I know for sure: God was always there. I just needed to know how to let him in." Arlene knows her calling: to act as midwife for women and their children as they embrace hope and discover new life.

Questions for Reflection and Discussion

- What are the events, decisions, and turning points that have shaped our life?
- How did Arlene's childhood experiences shape her future calling?
- How did forgiving help Arlene to heal?
- What are some of the boxes that hold us captive? How do we get out of them?

For Further Exploration

- How are the children in your community? What do our answers to this question say about the health, well-being, and attitudes of our communities and society?
- How do Jesus' words and example help us as we struggle to forgive? See Luke 6:37–38, 23:32–34.
- Why is hope important to life? What happens when an individual or a group feels as if they have no hope?
- In Exodus 1 and 2, both the Hebrew and Egyptian women acted in the struggle for freedom. Later in this book we shall read the story of Miriam, a prophet and a leader along with brothers Moses and Aaron. (Exodus 15:20–21; Numbers 12:1–16; Micah 6:4) What women do you remember as leaders in the struggle for freedom?

CHAPTER 3

Living the Prophetic Vision: Miriam and Jerry

Miriam's Story, Exodus 2:1–10, 15:20–21; Numbers 12:1–16; Micah 6:4

I am alone, shut out of the camp of my people, the source and ground of my life. Moses, the brother I rescued, has tried to silence me, but I have not lost my voice. I will sing my story, and the winds of the desert will carry my song to the daughters of my people.

And they will remember. They will remember the songs we sang together — songs of longing, of courage, of freedom.

I, with my brothers Moses and Aaron, led our people out of slavery, and now we are leading them safely through the merciless desert. But the journey is hard; hunger and thirst and the plague have been our journey-mates. When the desert threatens to overwhelm us, our people wail, "Why did we leave Egypt?"

Aaron and I, too, asked piercing questions, "Has the Lord spoken only through Moses? Has he not spoken through us also?"

So Moses, as if summoning all the power of the Lord, pointed his rod at me and roared, "Out! Out of the camp!" My skin turned leprous, white as snow, a warning to anyone who asks the hard questions. So I am alone, while inside the camp Aaron walks and speaks in freedom.

I have not always been alone; I have not always been silenced. I kept watch for the midwives who defied Pharaoh to save our sons. I sang the birthing songs to the women who labored in secret, hidden from the violence of the king's men. I schemed with wives and daughters of our masters when they dared to rescue our babies. To save my infant brother, Moses, I helped our mother, Jochebed, plaster a basket of rushes with tar. The watertight ark was his bed while we trusted in goodness and mercy. I watched for the princess, Meroe, the protector of children. So together we sang our secret songs, the daughters of Egypt and the daughters of Sarah — songs of rescue, songs of life.

When we were ready to leave Egypt, we invited Meroe to journey with us to the land of freedom. She said, "I must stay with my people," but she will live in the songs we sing and the stories we tell. Every time we offer hospitality in our new land, we will be remembering and honoring her. She will have a new name, Bityah, "Daughter of God."[1]

So we marched out of Egypt, beginning the road to freedom. We were old men and old women who had lost our youth to the greed of the king. We were children, dancing with wild excitement, running and leaping into a new adventure. We were mothers cradling infants, now safe in our embrace. We were fathers and husbands, heading for a land where we can be the protectors of our children. Slung on our shoulders we carried the bread that had no time to rise, bread that will be our bread of remembrance.

In the lead, I marched with my brothers, the death rumble of chariots and the beating hooves of the warrior horses closing in upon us. The power of Egypt pursued us while above us glowered the beasts of fear and death. But around us, before us, behind us was the Lord who had heard our cries and known our pain.

At our first steps into the water, the sea opened itself to us. When the bed of mud threatened to trap us, we lifted our feet high and pushed forward. The strong lifted the faltering, and the children pushed aside the reeds that blocked the paths of those who were blind.

When our people had crossed the dry shore, we watched in dread as our enemies reached the sea. But the sea was no friend to our pursuers. Their powerful horses lost their footing in the thick slime and threw their riders into the sea. The heavy chariots, Pharaoh's pride in war, turned over and sank, mired in the mud. We heard the horses' screams, the warriors' curses, and their desperate pleas to their gods.

So the songs of our women turned to songs of triumph. We danced, losing ourselves in ecstasy. Our feet flew faster and faster as we twirled to the beat of the tambourines. Laughter and rejoicing exploded in the camp. Our praise rose to the Lord God of freedom. If God is a dancing god, the Lord too must have moved with exhilaration, tapping holy feet with the beat of our songs.

> *Sing to the Lord, for he has triumphed gloriously;*
> *horse and rider he has thrown into the sea.*
> Exodus 15:21

But I wondered, "Does the Lord rejoice in the death of our enemies? Do our pursuers hate us, or are they, too, slaves to the greed and power of the king?"

As we journey through the harsh wilderness, we follow a pillar of cloud by day and a pillar of fire by night. But wherever we go, my well, the well my people call Miriam's well, travels with us.[3] When my people are thirsty, they drink deeply and are satisfied. When their spirits lag, when they beg us to lead them back to Egypt, where they were secure in their bondage, I offer them the cool, clear, sparkling water from my well and I can see again the light in their eyes and the strength of their wills.

As we travel, our songs give us strength and lift our spirits. At night our women lead as we sing and dance and tell our stories. We sing our praises to the god of freedom.

But now I sing alone, without the voices of my women to push away the dark and to drown out the moaning of the desert winds. I sing of loneliness and of fear. No one travels the merciless desert alone. Who would not watch with terror as darkness overwhelms the light?

In the distance, inside the camp, I can hear voices raised in command, in shock, and in anger. I can hear the cries of infants, the screams of women in labor. What I do not hear is merriment — the sounds of singing and dancing. I hear my women singing a lament for me, and I return their song. I beg of you, winds of the desert, carry my song to them.

But I hear no preparations for the journey onward. And I know I will not. My people will not leave without me, without my well, without my song. I am part of my people, and they are part of me. We are a web that cannot be broken.

I will go on asking the hard questions. I must; if I do not, who will? Can the people move on without their prophets? Can the people dream? Can the people sing of freedom, of joy, of hope if they do not know their stories? I will sing our songs; I will tell our stories. This is my calling. This is my gift.

1. For the story of Meroe, I am indebted to Sandy Eisenberg Sasso, *But God Remembered*, pp. 19–22.
2. See "Miriam's Song, Miriam's Silence," pp. 141–142, *The Women's Torah Commentary*, ed. Rabbi Elyoe Goldstein.

Jerry's Story

Freedom from oppression for all God's children — this is the dream of today's women who are walking in the footsteps of Miriam. They may be members of our congregations; they may be our own friends or our neighbors; they may even be chance acquaintances we meet on the street. Few will make headlines, launch new movements, or receive coveted prizes for their leadership. Yet they are faithful to the call to "do justice" and they challenge us to join them.

Jerry's graying hair and slight stoop mark her as one of the wise mothers of Kwanzaa. Her eagerness to meet and greet visitors tells them that there are no strangers at Kwanzaa. Before I recognized her as "Miriam," we had chatted about mutual friends, about happenings at the church, and about her amazing grandchildren. (Isn't that the privilege of grandparents?) Later, when we began to talk about her life, I knew why Reverend Alika named her as our Miriam.

Jerry knew racism as a young girl growing up in a racially mixed neighborhood in a city in Tennessee. Her best friend, Shirley, was white. She remembers the fun they shared when she slept over with her friend. Shirley's house had a sleeping porch where the girls could giggle, eat, and tell secrets away from the eyes and ears of adults.

Jerry's house, too, had something special for the neighborhood children — television! Jerry's father had several jobs and had been given the set at one of them. The television stood at a window and the neighborhood children, Black and white, gathered to watch. It was some time before Jerry's parents discovered that her enterprising brother, Kenneth, was charging admission — a nickel a child — for space on the grass outside the window!

Jerry was a young child when she first faced the reality of discrimination in her own neighborhood. The local ice cream parlor was a favorite place for children. There, for only a nickel each, she and Shirley could buy cones with their favorite flavors. One day everything changed. The owner, Miss Dooley, who was white and lived down the street from Jerry's family, announced to her young customer, "You can't sit down here!"

Jerry, just as determined, answered, "If Shirley can, I can. If I can't, she can't."

"I'm going to tell your mama on you," warned Miss Dooley. That was the first, but not the only, threat Jerry would receive and ignore.

On a very hot day the two girls decided that they were not going to sit outside in the blazing sun and let their ice cream melt. So they moved inside and, sitting together under the counter, licked their ice cream. It was a step toward justice taken by two young girls.

Jerry learned more about the difference in privilege when she started school. On the first day she expected Shirley to be in her class, but Shirley was missing. After school she asked her parents, "How come I'm not going to Shirley's school? How come she's not going to my school?" They had to explain to a five-year-old child the realities of the life she must face.

Jerry describes herself as "a difficult kid." She says, "If the sign on the water fountain said Whites Only, I didn't care. If I was thirsty, I was going to drink from it." She was taking small but real steps toward justice.

She was no more than twelve when she joined the Civil Rights Movement. Her family lived close to downtown, so one day while she was browsing in a dress shop, someone shouted from the door, "Come on over to Woolworth's and sit at the counter." The shop owner, like Miss Dooly, warned, "I'm going to tell your mother." Ignoring the threat, Jerry joined the others at the sit-in. "I didn't care," she says. "It was right even if I got into trouble."

"It was right" became her guide for living. Church was central in Jerry's family life. She remembers that Sundays were dedicated to church — all day long. There was morning worship; there were afternoon Sunday school classes; and in the evening they were back in church for another service. Church helped to shape her and to help her decide whether or not "it was right."

When Jerry was still in elementary school, a single tragic event ended the life the family had known. Her father, a chauffer, survived a crash that totaled the car and left him with a life-changing brain injury and damaged kidneys. For her mother it meant continuing care for the thirty-seven years he lived after the crash. For Jerry it was like losing one parent. Jerry remembers that after his brain injury, her father related to her like a child. She remembers playing childish games with him and describes herself as sometimes being "mean," grabbing something he was holding and running away while he chased her.

The time for childlike play passed, and Jerry's life as a typical teenager and high school student ended when she discovered that she was pregnant. Her pregnancy forced her to make hard decisions that would shape her own future and change the lives of those who were closest to her. The baby's father, who was also a teenager, was sent away by his family to escape a shotgun wedding. Jerry's mother was firm that she could not afford another child. She insisted on an abortion. She said, "You will go to school, and you are not to tell anyone."

Jerry's sister's boyfriend volunteered to take her to what she calls a "backwoods place," but Jerry knew how dangerous that could be. Finally, recognizing Jerry's determination, her mother promised, "I won't make you do it."

Jerry's sister and her fiancé offered another solution: they would take the baby. But Jerry was determined not to give up her child. Finally her mother said, "If you can prove to me that you can take care of your baby, you can keep it."

Jerry had worked for another family, so she knew how to baby-sit, cook, and clean. With that experience she dropped out of school, went to work, and began to set money aside to support her child. It was a difficult time for Jerry, but she remembers finding comfort and strength in prayer. "I knew God would save me," she says.

After a long and difficult delivery, her beloved Tammie was born. The infant was healthy but Jerry struggled to live. She remained in the hospital for days.

While she was fighting for her life, she saw herself get out of bed and go to the window. Looking out on the courtyard of the hospital, she saw her sister's fiancé, Bill, lying in a hospital bed and hooked up to tubes. She saw his mother there, wearing a peach colored sweater. Jerry saw him take his last breath. "Even today I can see it," she says.

When Jerry called home to ask about Bill, her mother denied that he was in the hospital. Trying to spare her sick daughter more pain, she directed the hospital to stop all telephone calls to Jerry and to admit no visitors.

Jerry was discharged and, at first, her family still refused to answer her questions about Bill. When they finally had to admit the truth, her fear was confirmed. Bill had died, but in a wing of the hospital far from the room where Jerry was struggling for her own life.

Jerry recovered, but her experience left her with another kind of struggle. It took many years for her to come to terms with what had happened to her. "I used to blame myself, thinking that my prayers did this," she says. "I loved God but was afraid to talk about it. I thought bad things might happen." Even as she struggled with self-blame she knew that "I still had to be the best person I could be."

After many years she was able to come to peace with the experience. Now she can affirm, "God doesn't make bad things happen." She believes that there is a plan — God's plan — and that events in our lives happen as part of that plan. She adds that the wisdom she finally gained is "one of the ways I've been able to deal with death. I think I see it differently from most people."

Jerry says that she has told her children, "If I die tonight, I've had a good life. God has prepared a place for me. He would not prepare a bad place for me."

Jerry married and had three more children, even though the doctor had told her she would not be able to get pregnant. Jerry's independent nature did not fit her husband's wish for a submissive stay-at-home wife. She could not be that kind of wife.

"I fought back," she says. She devised a plan, a way out of a marriage that had become abusive. She finally persuaded her husband to let her go to work, but he made it very clear that she would continue to do all the cooking, cleaning, shopping — everything, including doing their daughters' hair. Hard as it was, working outside the home made it possible to plan an escape and a future for herself and her children. When she could take care of her family, they would leave.

Her first attempt failed. One day while her husband was at work, she packed for herself and the children and ran to her mother's home. They did not receive a warm welcome. Her mother directed Jerry to return to her husband.

Even when her husband came after the family, dragged them away, and forced them back into his house, she knew they would leave again. "I decided that was not the way to do it," she says. She resolved that the next time, they would escape to their own home.

She rented a house and made a second attempt to escape. When the house went up in flames, the family survived but lost everything. (Ironically, the first responder was her husband's brother.) Again, Jerry and the children took refuge in her mother's home. Again, her husband came to her mother's home and demanded that Jerry stop the divorce proceedings. When the case went to court, the judge denied Jerry's plea for freedom.

For the third time, Jerry planned her escape, but with the advice of a good lawyer. He counseled her to return to her husband but to document what she did everyday and the actions of her husband. When she was ready, she filed again. This time, the judge granted her divorce.

She still remembers the "amazing" support she received as she and her children began their new life. As soon as their house was renovated after the fire, friends and even her supervisor at work gathered to help with the move. She reflected that the divorce finally gave her the ability to concentrate on raising her children.

One of the wishes for her children was to live in a better neighborhood. She moved her family to a white suburb. A telephone call shattered her illusions. After school one day her children called her at work, crying because neighborhood children were pounding on their door and threatening to kill them. After Jerry rushed home, she walked through the neighborhood and stopped to talk with each parent. She was sure they had been aware — and permissive — of their children's behavior. She told them that she had to work and could not be home all the time. "But," she informed them, "my children are not going to be tortured." She threatened action if the children were ever harmed in any way. "I'm going back to work, and I don't want anybody to ring my doorbell!"

Her instructions to the children were equally firm and clear: "Don't let anybody come in the door unless I'm home." This was the rule even when the neighborhood children invited her children to come outside and ride their three-wheelers. Later, a group of parents visited Jerry, apologized, and assured her that her children were safe.

Not long after, a bold move Jerry calls a "turning point" marked a new beginning for the family. Her parents and brother had moved to Minnesota, where he had a football scholarship at the university. Her mother urged Jerry to join them, arguing that the schools were good and that it was a good place to raise children. So with children from eight to twelve years of age, the young family embarked on what Jerry calls "a total change."

In Minneapolis she and the children had much to learn. Shortly after the move, her mother asked her to help remove the screens from the windows of her home. Jerry could not imagine why. Her mother explained that they would replace the screens with storm windows. In a moment of enlightenment, Jerry asked, "You mean it gets that cold here?"

Riding the bus was a challenge for both mother and children. The children had to overcome their fear of riding school buses, and Jerry had to learn to navigate the city with public transportation. Taking the bus to a job interview just a short distance from her parents' home, she became confused, and instead of riding the bus for a few minutes, she walked for two hours to reach her destination. In spite of the changes she and the children had to make, Jerry describes the move as a blessing. She says, "I had to have civility for myself and the kids."

The determination that Jerry brought to her personal and family life enabled her to cross some of the racial barriers to employment. After she decided to move to Minnesota, she asked her employer, Sears, for a transfer. She was told that this was against company policy, but when she applied in Minneapolis, she discovered that a glowing letter had already been sent on her behalf. "We've never received a recommendation like yours," they told her.

Sears could offer her only part-time work at first. But when they discovered that a suburban bank was trying to hire her, a position in the jewelry department opened up. There, she could work the hours she needed to support her family. Soon another opportunity was offered: furniture sales, which meant earning bigger commissions. The offer came with a warning: "They don't like women." Her response was, "I can deal with anyone!" She still needed extra income, so she took a second job, working part-time as a cashier in a store across the street from Sears.

After five years at Sears she felt that she needed a change. A friend sent her name and contact information to the Honeywell Corporation, and the very evening after he received it, a human resources person phoned and hired her! That was the beginning of a long career at Honeywell, where she worked until she retired after twenty-three years.

If Jerry had any illusions about escaping racism by moving to Minnesota, she was to learn that prejudice persisted there as in the state she left. Still she did not back away from saying what needed to be said. But she did so with skill and even forgiveness.

She was dating a white man when his sister "uninvited" Jerry to her wedding. When Katrina, the sister's eight-month-old baby was diagnosed with cancer, Jerry was the only person other than the mother who could hold and comfort the child. On the day Katrina died, Jerry, without knowing why, bought coffee and doughnuts to take to Katrina's home. They were ready for friends and family who arrived that evening. Forgiveness and reconciliation had become real — more than words, more than ideals.

Like Miriam, Jerry has known the "dark night of the soul." She was "feeling lost in family problems" when she first visited Kwanzaa. She invited family members to go with her but determined, "If no one will go with me, I'll go alone." Convinced as she was that she wanted to visit, she still did not expect to become part of the Kwanzaa family. She now believes, "God had a different plan."

Describing that first visit she says, "It was like God was using me. He was talking to me, comforting me. I wondered, 'What is going on?' I was expecting to feel something, but this was more than I could imagine." All she could say was, "Thank you, Jesus."

This sense of gratitude helps Jerry to live with assurance. She names the many losses she has experienced: two parents, two sisters, two brothers, and very recently, a granddaughter and her best friend. When I ask how she could handle so many losses, she says, "It's part of the journey. God is with me, holding my hand." She lives with the faith that God has them and that they are waiting to welcome her when her time comes. She says that when she needs to talk with her mother, "I ask God to put me through."

One way Jerry is coping with her latest losses is to start college. At first the idea was overwhelming. "I can't do this," she said. Her daughter Maurena's response was, "How do you know what you can or can't do until you try?" So Jerry, retiree and grandmother embarked on a new journey: college.

Reflecting on her life, Jerry describes it as an ever-expanding web. She believes that God is calling her to reach out beyond the web that begins with family, friends, and church, to touch the lives of others, including people she meets on the street.

She describes an encounter with a woman she met for the first time. Jerry sensed that she was in pain. Taking her hand Jerry asked, "Are you okay?" She offered to pray for her. She then discovered that the woman's daughter had lupus. Jerry adds that she tells people whose lives she touches, "I don't need to know your story. That is between you and God."

Jerry continues the work for justice she began as a young girl sitting-in at the ice cream parlor. She related the story of a conversation with Katrina's grandfather, whose words and actions had shown how deeply prejudiced he was. She told him, "If you want my respect, you've got to change."

To her charge he replied, "This is how I grew up. I know in my heart I don't want to feel some of the things I feel. Because of you, I'm working on it." Jerry grew up facing the racism that still pervades our society, but she reaches out with love and concern and honesty — and with the skill to articulate what she believes and what she stands for.

Jerry says that she is on her knees in prayer as soon as she awakes every morning. She is grateful for the people God sends her and who become part of her life: "God has put me in touch with people who need me. He has other things for me to do. He's not done with me yet." This is the faith that has sustained her during a long life and that has made it possible for her to offer friendship, concern, and challenge to the expanding web of persons whose lives are changed because of her ministry.

When Miriam was put outside the camp, the people of Israel could not move on. Without our prophets, can we as congregations, as communities, as a society move on? Without the prophets among us, will our churches "welcome the stranger"? Will our children be safe? Will any of us be truly free?

Like the young girl we call Miriam, Jerry knew, at a very young age, that she could not submit to evil. When she stood up to the mothers who were allowing their children to bully Black children, she was challenging the ways racism is passed on through generations. When she continues to confront acquaintances whose attitudes perpetuate oppression, she is calling each of us to examine our own hearts and lives.

No, we cannot move on without our prophets who have a vision of what God wants for our world. We cannot move on without the prophets who stand beside and before us, calling us to be faithful even when we are weary. Thanks be to God for those who live by the words of the Hebrew prophet, "to do justice, and to love kindness, and to walk humbly with your God." (Micah 6:8)

Questions for Reflection and Discussion

- Who are the prophetic voices in your life, in your church, in your community?
- What is the response to the persons you named?
- How does your church carry on a prophetic ministry?
- In your own "dark night of the soul," what sustained you?

For Further Exploration

- Do you agree with the writer's interpretation of Miriam's story?
- Miriam's story was told by men from the perspective of Moses. How might it be told differently today?
- What causes people — both women and men — to be "outside the camp" today? Who are the marginalized in our society?
- What hope is there for welcoming people who are marginalized into the camp?
- How have people in oppressed groups survived? You may wish to use other stories in this collection to think about this question.
- Is there a difference between a prophetic ministry and showing compassion or doing good?

CHAPTER 4

Living the Presence: Deborah, Doris, Iesha, and Regina

Deborah's Story, Judges 4:4–10

Tomorrow I will lead my people into battle. I will lead with the strength of a mother protecting her children. I will go where my people go.

My people come to me each day for counsel as I sit under the sacred tree they call the palm of Deborah. I shoulder the burden of their disputes: sheep stolen in the night, boundary markers lost, and marriage agreements broken. I measure guilt and mete out justice. Always I speak as a prophet, proclaiming the wisdom of God and reminding the people that we are called to be a holy people and to live with righteousness and justice.

Beneath these stories there is a deeper pain; my people are not free. Where there should be singing and dancing, there is crying in the night. Dark shadows of fear and anger cloud the eyes that once glowed with hope. I have heard the stories of grain destroyed, of wives and daughters ravished, of young men mutilated. My people are afraid to travel to our shrines. They must arm themselves as they work in the fields, wrestling life from the unwilling ground.

But my people's stories of pain are not our only stories. We have another story to tell. In the days of Moses and Miriam, our God bore our people out of slavery as on the wings of eagles. Our God is a deliverer, a liberating God.

So I laid my plans and summoned Barak. At first he hesitated. He spoke with measured words: "Only if you go with me will I go." Was he trembling before the power of the Canaanites? Was he challenging me, saying that only if I dared to risk my own life would he risk his? Or was he testing my determination, doubting the courage of a woman?

I will lead my people because I am a mother of Israel. Our foremothers — Sarah, Rebecca, Rachel, Leah — gave birth to sons. I will birth a free people. I will go with them.

Doris' Story

When I ask Doris to choose a biblical woman for her story, she does not hesitate. "Deborah!" Whether she is organizing a church supper, entertaining her deacon's "family," or giving sought after advice, Doris has been a wise and dependable presence for both her Kwanzaa family and her biological family. Her life has fulfilled the promise of Deborah, "I will surely go with you." (Judges 4:9)

Doris describes herself as "a strong woman." As the oldest of twelve children, she learned to be responsible at a very young age. She was eighteen when her father died, leaving her mother with twin boys who were three weeks old.

In spite of the challenges of their big family, Doris remembers her mother as being "very particular about getting an education." The children lived up to their mother's high expectation. Every one attended college except one brother who chose carpentry as his profession. Doris herself attended Wilberforce College in Ohio for two years.

Doris' marriage to Arneuwell and their move from Indianapolis to Minneapolis did not end her responsibility for her family. When her mother was diagnosed with breast cancer, she came to Minnesota to be treated at the Mayo Clinic. She stayed with Doris' family, and they drove back and forth between home and Rochester until Doris took her mother back to the family home in Indianapolis to die.

Doris describes her mother's death as a "turning point" because it gave her new insight into her own life. Six children — three boys and three girls — were still at home when their mother died. The youngest was only fourteen. Doris and one of her brothers had to assume responsibility for their younger siblings. Doris had a six-month-old baby when her mother died, but she made many trips to Indianapolis. "I had to take on the role of the mother," she says. "I always had to do more than the average person. Someone had to be there. I had to be a Deborah."

Doris' first job in Minneapolis was working on an assembly line in a Honeywell plant. Soon, however, she got a job as a reservation agent for Northwest Airlines. Doris and Arneuwell raised three children — daughters Larissa and Evony and son Rodney — while she was working for the airline.

I ask about her work experience, whether she faced racism on her job. She answers that she had trouble with only one supervisor, a woman who was angry because her daughter was dating a Black man. Doris, a daughter of Deborah, stood up to the woman's abuse. "I will not accept this from you. I won't be treated this way!"

Doris remembers coworkers asking, "How did you get this job?" When I ask how she answered, she treats me to her infectious laugh, and tells me, "My personality!" She feels that she was able to get along with "most" of her coworkers. She says that they knew she was very active in her church and respected her for that.

Her retirement in 2000 and Arneuwell's retirement from the Metropolitan Airport Commission in 2006 did not mean settling into a leisurely life style. In 1998 they had taken responsibility for the care of two grand nephews. Joshua was two months and Thomas was fifteen months when they came to live with Doris and Arneuwell.

She describes raising children as "making sure the younger ones get what they need." She places a high value on education, and one of her priorities for the children is seeing that they get the education they need. Her husband shares her passion for education, having served fourteen years on the school board of Brooklyn Center, the suburb where they lived for forty years.

At Kwanzaa each deacon has a "family" for which the deacon assumes leadership. According to one Kwanzaa member, "Everyone wants to be in Deacon Doris' family." Acclaimed as one of Kwanzaa's best cooks, she entertains the twenty-plus family members in her home. In addition she always does what she calls "something special" for the holidays.

Doris expects members of her "family" to be in church regularly. If they miss Sunday worship, Doris telephones to see whether there is a problem. She calls to "chat" but also asks, "Can I pray for you?" Sometimes she hears about problems or questions she needs to refer to a pastor.

Doris' joy is her church. Along with the sociability, she loves the ways she can serve. Doris' culinary skills are not limited to her deacons' family. Every summer Kwanzaa sponsors a six- to eight-week Freedom School.[1] Doris has been one of two chefs who plan and prepare daily lunches (spaghetti, lasagna, chili — favorite kids' meals) for 125 to 150 students and staff. She admitted that her family wants her to slow down. Her response? "I'm not done yet!" She says that she gets "too excited" about what she is doing. "People know that what I do comes from my heart."

Knowing that others respect and look up to her creates a unique challenge for Doris. "I want to make sure I'm doing the right thing. I don't always know if I'm giving the right advice. I can't always give them what they want. Sometimes I can't do anything. The challenge is 'insight,' to give the right advice or to refer them to the pastors. The most important thing is to pray."

Where does Doris find the inner resources to be a Deborah — leader, advisor, and wise presence? Her prayer for herself is for strength, but she takes comfort in the assurance that besides her own life of prayer, the pastors are praying for her. For the many to whom she has given so much, her prayerful presence is the greatest gift.

1. *Freedom Schools are African-American literacy programs for children and teenagers. They were founded by civil rights workers to supplement the "separate but equal" schools that were separate but not equal. They are now held in cooperation with the Children's Defense Fund. Kwanzaa is one of two Freedom Schools that serve high schoolers as well as elementary-age children. In addition to improving their reading skills, students meet community leaders and participate in community service.*

Iesha's Story

In a large public hospital in Minneapolis, Dr. Iesha wages a daily battle for the lives and well being of her patients. A modern Deborah, her enemies are not warring tribes but diseases, many of which are linked to poverty or lack of adequate continuing health care. Her weapons are wisdom, commitment to her patients, and many years of training.

Many of her patients are new Americans, persons who have come seeking better lives, or, too often, to escape warfare or torture in their home countries. As Dr. Iesha meets with them, she often explains the diagnosis and treatment through an interpreter. The translator may be fluent in Spanish or in Hmong or in Somali or in any of the other twenty languages for which the hospital provides interpreters.[1]

Poverty and racism have pushed many of Dr. Iesha's patients to the margins of society. Many come in fear because of the long history of abuse or neglect by some medical practitioners. Memories of the syphilis research performed on African-American men at Tuskegee are still very much alive.[2]

Most patients, whether they are new Americans or long-term residents, are struggling to find their way through the tangle of a complex and often confusing medical system. It is into this setting that Dr. Iesha has been called. But whomever she is treating, she knows how essential it is for them to bring their own spiritual resources to the process of healing.

Iesha was only seven years old when she knew she wanted to be a doctor. Her baby sister, Iyana, was very sick and had to be hospitalized for several weeks. "I wanted to be someone who makes babies better."

Now a specialist in internal medicine, Iesha envisions new ways to be present with her patients. "You can't separate the spiritual from the physical. The two need to be incorporated in treatment," she says. She admits that this can be difficult because so much depends upon the patient's belief system. Nevertheless, she believes that doctors need to be trained for integrating spirituality into traditional medicine.

Iesha is on the staff of the Hennepin County Medical Center (HCMC) in Minneapolis. She has chosen to work with underserved patients. She summarizes the hospital's mission statement as "providing care to patients who don't have a ton of money." Patients at HCMC come from many different countries and represent broad cultural diversity. Most depend on medical assistance. Her own values and the complexity of the challenges attracted her to HCMC. In addition HCMC is a teaching hospital. "I like teaching a lot," she says. "It helps me stay fresh."

As for the future, she says, "I'll see where God wants me to be." One thing she is sure of is that she wants to be able to integrate the medical and the spiritual. "That is where I will go," she says.

According to Iesha, her values in practicing medicine reflect the values of her parents, both of whom are Presbyterian ministers. She describes her childhood as "normal, nothing like what people imagine life to be like for preachers' kids." She recalls that she never felt the pressure to be perfect.

When she was growing up, her family life presented some unique challenges. Iesha was born in Minneapolis, where her father was the pastor of a large congregation. When she was three, the family moved to Atlanta, where sister Iyana was born. In Atlanta both parents pursued graduate studies. Her father earned a Doctor of Ministry and her mother earned her Master of Divinity at the Interdenominational Theological Center. It was necessary for her parents to live apart during some of this time. The children lived with their mother for one year in Atlanta and with their father for three years in North Carolina.

When Iesha was in the tenth grade, the family returned to Minneapolis. Iesha remembers experiencing "culture shock" and "weather shock." In comparison with the southern states, Minnesota has few African-American residents. In addition, Iesha says that she had to get used to the way Minnesotans speak.

When she graduated from North High School in Minneapolis, her outstanding ACT scores qualified her for the most select colleges. From the schools that courted her, she chose Stillman College, one of the Historically Black Colleges and Universities. Besides recognizing its fine academic programs, Iesha knew that she needed to be in a "nice environment." She says, "I'm a visual person." After visiting several campuses, she chose "beautiful" Stillman.

From Stillman Iesha went on to medical school at the University of Cincinnati. She faced tough challenges but says, "My upbringing helped because my parents had passed on their values, had helped me learn confidence and perseverance. It fueled my ability to make it."

Iesha had expected to specialize in pediatrics, but she discovered, during a rotation in internal medicine,[3] that she enjoyed working with adults and the relationships she was able to form with them.

Solid training in medicine was not all Iesha found in medical school. There, she met her husband, Kevin, her "best friend." Kevin, a family practice physician, shares Iesha's passion for bringing good health care to people who have been marginalized. He is on the staff of the NorthPoint Health & Wellness Center whose mission is " ... providing culturally appropriate, integrated, holistic primary health and social services."

A new challenge for Iesha and Kevin arrived on November 26, 2011, with the birth of Inara Sakai. Her name means "Heaven-sent daughter" and "Brings her parents joy." Iesha says, "I love her more than anything. She is the greatest gift — just a blessing." Speaking of the ways the baby may change her parents' lives, she says, "I don't know yet what will come. I have to navigate through sleeplessness and get some brain function back." Describing her hope for her child, Iesha says her wish is that she will "be happy" and "fulfill whatever is her purpose in life." Inara Sakai follows several generations of purposeful women: Dr. Iesha, grandmother, and great-grandmother who was the first Black woman elected as president of a school board in California.

Judge, counselor, warrior — Deborah brought a wise and strong presence to her people as they struggled for life in a new land. Centuries later in a changing medical system, Dr. Iesha, a strong and wise modern Deborah, is committed to excellent medical care for all persons including the "least of these." (Matthew 25:40) To her work she brings the best modern medicine and more — her sensitivity to the spiritual resources of her patients. She is drawing not only on the strength of Deborah; she is also reclaiming the wisdom of the first-century Jewish healer who did not separate the physical and the spiritual, and who knew the healing power of the community.[4] In this century, Dr. Iesha is pointing the way for healing that honors both body and spirit.

1. Interpreters are available for Amharic, Arabic, ASL, Bosnian, Cantonese, Cambodian, French, German, Hmong, Laotian, Mandarin, Oromo, Portuguese, Russian, Somali, Spanish, Swahili, Taiwanese, Ukrainian, and Vietnamese.
2. In *The Immortal Life of Henrietta Lacks*, Rebecca Skloot tells the story of the cells taken, without consent, from the body of an African-American woman dying of cancer. The cells have been used worldwide by researchers and biotech companies. Among the many discoveries, the cells made possible the development of the polio vaccine. The family never shared in the wealth generated by the use of Henrietta's cells.

3. During their third and fourth years of medical school, students do six-week hospital rotations in major medical fields and also have the opportunity to choose rotations in fields of special interest.

4. Black, Kathy. *A Healing Homiletics: Preaching and Disability*, pp. 45–53

Regina's Story

Service to others and inner strength: these are at the core of Regina's ministry of presence. A modern Deborah, she is present with her people as friend, leader, teacher, and advisor. Her life experiences, often working with "the least of these," have prepared her for the trusted roles she holds in her north Minneapolis community and in the service agencies where she works.

Regina was born in a small town in Iowa. When she was nine, her family moved to Minneapolis, hoping for better employment opportunities for her father. They lived with other family members until they moved into a housing project in north Minneapolis, the community where Regina still finds her "heartbeat." All did not go well, however. Regina's father had a drinking problem, and her mother, who had not been working outside the home, went to work as a housekeeper.

When Regina was nineteen, she gave birth to a son. He was only a year and a half when it was discovered that he had leukemia. He outlived his doctor's expectations but died when he was four. Regina says that in spite of her terrible grief, she has always been grateful for the time she had him in her life.

Three months before her child died, Regina made a decision that radically changed her life. She accepted Christ as her Lord and Savior. She had been using drugs, but her faith, along with therapy, gave her the support and courage to give them up. In her words, she "married spiritual strength with therapy" by "combining spirituality with the natural." When she had to face the death of her child, she found the strength to move through the searing pain. She had begun a long spiritual journey.

Events on the national and local scenes were also shaping Regina's life and future. In the early 1970s, racial turmoil shook north Minneapolis. Job opportunities began to open up for African Americans. Regina found a job as a receptionist at The Way, a north Minneapolis center for advocacy and service. She recalls, "The Way allowed me the opportunity to get involved in the community." This was the beginning of her many years of community service.

Regina was struggling, both through her own personal spiritual journey and her community involvement, to discover who she was as an African-American woman. At the same time, she was growing in her identity as a Christian. She joined the Black Panthers but soon discovered that the group was not right for her.

She changed jobs to work at a nonprofit law firm. Her interest in her new position came out of a past desire to work as a criminal lawyer. "I wanted to be part of the empowerment for those who were struggling for their legal rights," Regina says. She credits her involvement with the justice system as influencing her future ministry. As she worked with clients, she could see their need for a relationship with God. "My heartbeat was to see people come to Christ."

At the legal rights center she met her first husband. A year later the first child of their marriage was born. She and her husband shared a deep desire to bring others to Christ. Together they opened a Christian coffeehouse in downtown Minneapolis. There they led Bible studies with a strong emphasis on discipleship.

Regina knew that she had to act on the passionate concern she felt for the teens they met who were trading sex. She and her husband began to work with the juvenile justice system, advocating for the young women. They even became foster parents for some of the girls. But they shared a vision of doing more, a dream of opening a halfway house, where the young women could live in safety and receive the support they needed to get out of prostitution.

Their dream took on reality when, with the help of area churches, they purchased a large house in south Minneapolis for their ministry with women, then a second building where they could extend their ministry to men. The next stage of ministry was starting a new church in the community where they were working.

Along with the joy and challenge of ministry, there was sadness. Regina says that the spousal relationship lacked balance. She and her husband were so busy meeting the needs of others that they failed to meet their own. After twenty-five years, the marriage ended in divorce.

It was time for Regina to pursue her own spiritual growth. She broadened her ministry as she traveled internationally, speaking of her love for Christ in Rome, London, Kenya, and Seoul. In Africa she was ordained to an interdenominational ministry. She became the Reverend Regina!

She returned to Minnesota and went back to north Minneapolis. She is convinced that even though she was disconnected from the community she loved during the twenty-five years of her first marriage, God had given her a heartbeat for north Minneapolis. "I was gone for a time but when the season was complete, I returned."

With her return to north Minneapolis, Regina began to study the seven principles of Kwanzaa: unity, self-determination, collective works and responsibility, cooperative economics, purpose, creativity, and faith. She explains that among African-American Christians, there is much misunderstanding about Kwanzaa, that many believe that the principles are opposed to Christianity. As she studied she discovered that the principles were compatible with her beliefs and life as a Christian. Regina's new understanding freed her to attend Kwanzaa Church. She remembers losing friends because of her decision, but she says, "I needed to be fed."

At Kwanzaa Regina's rich gifts were recognized. She often shared in worship leadership, bringing fresh insights to scripture. She says she had not lost her "open heart" for young women who were working the streets, so she went out into the streets to talk with them. "I told them that God loved them as they were but too much to leave them that way." (She adds that this is true for all of us. "We are always growing.")

Regina discovered that she could love again. She describes Ed as a "traditional husband" whose wish was to be the sole financial support of the family. The onset of Ed's cancer has made this impossible.

Regina divides her professional life between her own nonprofit agency, Life Changes, and Twin Cities RISE, where she works as the Empowerment Coordinator. She describes herself as a coach and a teacher. She works with clients on issues that include taking responsibility, making choices, and self-esteem. She says that others have tried to persuade her to earn a college degree. She has audited college classes but is not tempted by the financial benefits that would come with a degree.

Describing her mission at Life Changes, she says, "We are always going through the seasons of our lives. We walk with families through these transitions." She believes that for some families, poverty is at the root of everything else. Not all Regina's clients are poor, however. At a workshop, a corporate executive might share her or his life experience with a person whose life is being ground down by poverty. Life Changes, according to Regina, goes beyond symptoms to see the real person. She says that people from all walks of life go through the same struggles and that is why it is necessary to get beyond symptoms.

Regina describes her ministry as a "ministry of presence." "We must be willing to step into the person's life and speak their language," she says. "Too often we do not understand the language of those that God loves."

In contrast with much of popular Christianity, Regina does not condemn the people she serves, many of whom are trading sex, are homeless, or are living with HIV/AIDS. "Let them know they are loved. Let them know they are not alone."

Speaking of north Minneapolis she says, "God has not left this community." She dreams of opening a drop-in center where people can be introduced to Christ at their own level, where they can get their basic needs met. She uses the words of Jesus as he addressed those who had fed the hungry, given a drink to the thirsty, welcomed the stranger, clothed the naked, taken care of the sick, and visited those who were in prison: " ... just as you did it to one of the least of these who are members of my family, you did it to me." (Matthew 25:40) "This identifies my calling," she says.

Regina ministers to others out of her own experience that "to encounter the love of God can change our lives." In her journey through pain, by "living within the pain," she has found healing. She compared "living the pain" with the trauma of giving birth. After childbirth there is life! "The fruit of the pain," she says, "is to be the person God created me to be." She has found hope and it is in that hope that she lives.

Regina's strong presence is felt in the community she loves and in the agencies where she serves. Like her spiritual foremother, she can promise, "I will go with you." Leader, advisor, teacher — she is a modern Deborah.

Questions for Reflection and Discussion

- Think of someone who has been a presence in your life. In what ways has that person been present for you?
- In what ways are you present for another person? Remember, sometimes the best way to be present is to simply be with another and to listen without giving advice or judging.
- Each of the three modern women is a presence for her people. How are their ways of living the present alike, and how are they different?

For Further Exploration

- Review the stories of these three other strong biblical women: Rahab (Joshua 2:1–21), A Wise Woman (2 Samuel 20:1, 14–22), and Abigail (1 Samuel 25:1–42). What do the three have in common? How are they different?
- Name other strong women whose courage or wisdom saved her people.
- Each of the three modern women is a wise presence. What does wisdom mean today, and how do we attain it? See Psalms 37:30, 111:10; James 1:5, 3:13–18.

CHAPTER 5

Living Truth: Huldah and Deborah

Huldah's Story, 2 Kings 22–23:27

I have looked into the future and I am brokenhearted. In my dreaming, asleep or awake, I can hear the cries of my people. I can feel their pain. I will be a witness to the death of our kingdom. But is there hope for our children and for our children's children? Surely the God of hope, the God of the covenant has not abandoned us.

We have gathered today at the command of King Josiah. Old and young, great and small, weak and powerful — we are all together, standing before the temple. All is silent; it seems that even the wind has ceased its whispering.

I tremble as I relive, over and over, the day the king's men came to my home. They stood at my door, five powerful men, five who came with the might of the kingdom. I welcomed them, but they returned no greeting. Instead, five ashen faces, furrowed with deep lines of despair, looked back at me. Instead of their usual assurance of power, I saw shades of doom.

I was seized by terror. My first thought was "Arrest!" But my reason protested, "Why? There is no cause. My husband has served the temple faithfully as the keeper of the wardrobe." Nevertheless, there they were: Hilkiah, the high priest; Shaphan, the king's secretary; Shaphan's son Ahikam; Achbor, the king's officer; and the king's trusted servant Asaiah.

A new thought chilled me. You see, I am a prophet, and my calling is not an easy one. Speaking the truth does not make one welcome to those who most need to hear the truth. I glanced around, but I saw no soldiers, no guards.

Hilkiah drew a scroll from the folds of his robe. He broke the silence. "King Josiah has sent us. He said, 'Go, inquire of the Lord for me, for the people, and for all of Judah, concerning the words of the book that has been found; for great is the wrath of the Lord that is kindled against us, because our ancestors did not obey the words of this book, to do according to all that is written.'"

"Why have you come to me and not to the great prophet, Jeremiah?" I asked. The men exchanged furtive looks. I needed no other explanation. Everyone dreaded Jeremiah's harsh pronouncements. I knew this was a clue to what was written in the scroll. "Come in," I said. As if entry into my house was pulling the delegation deeper into a dark reality, they entered.

"Where did the scroll come from? Who found it?" I demanded.

"I discovered it," said Hilkiah, "as the workers were repairing the temple. Shaphan brought me money so the workers could pay for … "

"Yes, yes," I interrupted. "So you took the scroll to the king?"

"Yes," said Hilkiah. "I told Shapham, 'I have found the book of the law in the house of the Lord.' Together we went to the palace. When the king heard the words in the scroll, he wailed; he howled. Everyone in the palace heard and everyone — princes, women, servants — took up the howling. Above the cries, we heard the shrill voices of women, 'It is the Day of the Lord!' Finally, when the king had no more tears and his voice was hoarse, he sent us to you. You shall decide if the scroll is genuine or if it is a fraud."

He handed me the scroll. As I began to unroll it, its leather resisted, as if it did not want to give up its message. I began to read the ancient script. The words were like trumpets blaring out truths I did not want to know. My eyes clouded; my hands shook. But I could not stop; I read on.

The words spoke of the sacred covenant the Holy One had made with our ancestors. They told what the Holy One requires of us — to be a holy people as the Lord our God is holy. They called us to worship only the Lord and to love our neighbor. They forbade the sacrifice of our children. They commanded us to keep the Passover, remembering our ancestors' delivery from slavery.

As I read, scenes from the lives of our people broke into my thoughts. They keep household gods, pagan idols, in places of honor in many of their homes. Horses dedicated to the sun stand at the gates of the temple. Our people worship the sun and moon and stars on the very roof of the house of the Lord. Men still defy our ancient law by sacrificing their sons and daughters to earn favors from the gods. There has been no Passover since the days of the good King Hezekiah, many years ago.

I was terrified for our people. But could I speak? And why me? Why must I be the one? Why had the Holy One called me, a woman, to announce the doom of the people I loved?

I wanted to curse the hours I had spent as a child, learning my letters while other girls learned to bake and weave. If only I could have refused when the Holy One called me to be a prophet! I had pleaded my unworthiness, but the Lord of the universe would not let me go.

Could I soften the truth? Could I pretend that the scroll was a fraud? Could I claim not to understand the words?

I could speak the truth, or I could deny it. The choice was mine. Or was it? Perhaps it was for this time, above all other times, that I had been called. I remembered the words of another prophet, many years ago, "Here am I; send me." (Isaiah 6:8)

I had no choice. I had to reveal the truth that had been entrusted to me. The scroll was genuine, and I had to speak.

I had to still the pounding in my chest, but my voice was firm and clear. "Go and tell the king," I directed, "The Holy One says, 'I will indeed bring disaster on this place and its inhabitants — all the words that the king of Judea has read. Because they have abandoned me and made offerings to other gods ... my wrath will be kindled against this place.' But say to the king, 'Because your heart was penitent, and you humbled yourself before the Lord, you shall be gathered to your grave in peace.' "

The men who stood before me bowed their heads. As they turned to go, I saw tears on the cheeks of these proud men.

So today, the people of Judah are all here. The crowd, which would otherwise bustle with anticipation, is silent. As King Josiah reads the book of the covenant, I see men weeping openly. I see mothers enfolding children as if they can protect them.

Finally, at the end of the reading the king calls on the people to promise, as their ancestors did, to keep the covenant and to be faithful to the One who called them. The silence shatters as the crowd thunders, "We will!"

I know that King Josiah will try to turn away the future. He will order that idols be burned, that altars of foreign gods be destroyed. He will command the destruction of places of child sacrifice. He will proclaim a great Passover. But it is too late for this generation. Our beloved Jerusalem will be destroyed.

What of the future? Will we, as God promised Abraham, be a blessing to all the people of the world? Will we teach those who follow us to love God and neighbors? Will the words of our prophets call the world to justice for the oppressed? For the Holy One, death and destruction are not the final words. Our God is a god of hope.

Deborah's Story

What does it mean to speak the truth in a time and place far removed from the Jerusalem temple and the seventh century BCE? In our search for a modern Huldah, we discovered Deborah.

People who meet her for the first time may underestimate the courage and tenacity of this petite, soft-spoken woman. Deborah's faith calls her to be a truth-teller, to act on her faith every day of the week. Her life as a Christian is not a Sunday-only commitment. Like Huldah she must speak the truth, even when doing so causes tension, frustration, or pain.

Deborah speaks with passion about the truths that must be remembered, told, and passed on to each new generation — the stories of the suffering and struggles of African-American people. "It has been difficult," she says, "for the elders to tell their stories because they are so painful." She knows that one pair of grandparents fled the Klan in Louisiana, barely escaping lynching. Years later, Deborah's mother was sent to Louisiana to spend a summer. She remembers being "terrified," afraid that she would do or say something that would endanger herself or someone else.

Her other grandfather told the story of returning to Mississippi for a visit after his family had moved to California. The police stopped him and demanded that he prove that he owned the car he was driving. (The officers considered the car "too good" for a Black man.) Her grandfather had papers with proof of ownership with him, but they were not enough for the officer. Her grandfather had to call a white person in California to vouch for him. Speaking of those experiences, Deborah says, "I can't not take the opportunities I've been given. To do so would be disrespectful to my grandparents and my parents."

She is convinced that young people need to know the truth about the struggles of those who came before them, on whose shoulders they are standing. She urges youth not to throw away the opportunities for which others have paid so high a price. She believes that it is necessary for white and Black people to have an "honest conversation" about race. She sees herself as part of a continuing story and is determined to continue the story in a positive way.

Deborah's own story begins with good memories of her childhood in California. "I was blessed with a really nice family." She describes her family life as "normal, close, supportive — that has been a wonderful thing, a wonderful memory. So many didn't have that. I had the security of knowing I was loved." She says that in her parents, she saw " ... tangible evidence of God's love. My parents taught me what a lived faith is." Besides loving parents Deborah and her brother had the advantage of having grandparents who lived close to them in Richmond, California.

Along with many trips her family enjoyed together, Deborah remembers the dinners the family shared every evening. "This seems so basic — so fundamental to family life." Friends of Deborah and her brother knew about their family tradition of always eating together, even if dinner had to be very late. Deborah remembers friends calling late at night and asking, "So are you eating dinner?"

Deborah's parents were both graduates of the University of California in Berkeley. In addition, her mother earned a Master of Social Work from Columbia University. From her mother, Deborah got her love of reading. She remembers that her mother never went anywhere without a book, and Deborah began, very early, to read her mother's books. She was reading science fiction by Isaac Asimov when she was still in elementary school. Needless to say, Deborah's parents had high expectations for her and her brother. "If you can get into college, you are going!" they hold her.

Her parent's commitment to service shaped Deborah's life. "They were trying to make the world a better place for everyone." Her mother was a social worker for a children's hospital and once spent a summer in India teaching English. "I got my sense of adventure from my mother," she says.

Deborah's father was a truth-teller in the public arena. As human relations officer for Richmond, California, he exercised responsibility for enforcing compliance with equal opportunity regulations. When builders complained that they could not find minority contractors, he asked, "Where are you looking?" With passage of the Americans with Disabilities Act, he worked to guarantee justice for another group of marginalized citizens. (One can only imagine the compromises people of privilege tried to force upon him.) Deborah remembers not only the integrity he brought to his work but his detailed and lengthy explanations. Deborah says he always wanted to make sure his listeners understood.

He built a level of trust that made it possible to walk into dangerous situations and diffuse mounting violence. During periods of unrest, he often rode along with the police at night. Both the police and the Black Panthers trusted and respected him, so he was able to talk with both parties and keep peace. Deborah remembers her mother saying that she sat at home praying whenever he was out on the "ride alongs."

Deborah's father was a prolific writer, and his writings are part of the rich legacy he left for his family and community. Deborah believes that he expressed the meaning of his life and his commitment to service in an article the family included in the printed program for his memorial service in August 2012. "Perhaps the real goal in life should become growing in our knowledge of God and, in the process, growing in the knowledge of everything else we need to know."[1]

Deborah says, "My tribute to my father is becoming the woman I'm supposed to be."

Her parents' commitment to justice helped to open opportunities for young people in Deborah's generation. But when she entered college, she discovered that in spite of some progress African-American students still faced attitudinal barriers. The attitudes were not as extreme or as overt as what her parents had faced. Deborah recalls hearing her parents say that while they were in college, it was not uncommon for college admissions personnel to tell white applicants, "We can't let you in. We had to take a Black person."

Deborah enrolled at the University of California in Davis. There, she faced significant changes. About half of the student body at her high school were African Americans. At her college only about three percent were African Americans.

Deborah found support and recognition in professional organizations. The National Society of Black Engineers offered a peer group. The Math, Engineering, and Science Achievement Program encouraged women and other underrepresented groups to pursue careers in those fields. The Emerging Scholars Program (ESP), a calculus honors program, challenged Deborah and recognized her for her scholarship. After her second year of math, she worked as a teaching assistant for ESP until graduation. Deborah graduated from UCD with a Bachelor of Science in chemical engineering and went on to earn a Master of Science in chemical engineering at the University of California in Santa Barbara.

Deborah's big move was to Minnesota and to a position as a chemical engineer at 3M. Deborah says that her experience has been very different from that of her parents who were educated in the pre–Civil Rights era. Nevertheless, in spite of having earned a master's degree, she still encounters racial stereotypes. Coworkers still express occasional surprise at her ability, assuming that Affirmative Action means hiring underqualified workers!

Courage to tell the truth is essential in her work as a chemical engineer in a large multinational corporation. If you have ever purchased a product only to discover that you were duped by false advertising, you will understand the importance of truth-telling in business. Deborah is a liaison between the research lab whose job, she says, is "discovering truth" and the manufacturing division whose responsibility is translating new ideas into "truth in performance." "We have to be honest," she says.

Deborah describes her work as "scaling up" a dependable product for customers. For nonengineers, Deborah compares "scaling up" with baking a quiche. ("I'm a food person," she says.) "I always want to be able to explain what I do to my mother without using jargon."

Deborah explains, "If we know how to bake one quiche, how do we scale up to bake three quiches? Change the baking time? Change the temperature? In taking an idea from the lab, how do we make the idea work as it moves to manufacturing? How do we make sure we are making what the lab developed?" (Deborah works with car-care products for do-it-yourselfers. Scaling up may mean adapting an idea in order to make thousands or even millions of the new product.)

The process is not quick or easy. There are no shortcuts. The process takes time as engineers do multiple testing to verify the integrity of the product. "We need to make sure it is right."

Ensuring the integrity of a new product can cause tension between the commercial people who want it on the market as soon as possible and the technical people like Deborah. "I have to be truthful with myself and with others. If there's an issue, I need to be honest." She explains that rushing the process can cost many thousands of wasted dollars and produces an inferior product for customers.

Truth-telling can be difficult and threatening, but Deborah knows, and coworkers agree, that she has a rare gift for saying what needs to be said. "I need to explain this in a way people can hear," she says. "This means understanding who and where they are and what kind of explanation they need. This includes being able to hear their legitimate suggestions."

Deborah's gift for engaging in the hard conversations extends beyond her professional life. People come to her because they know she will listen. "When you can say what they need to hear in a gentle

63

way, they will come back." She recalls a conversation with a man who claimed to not believe in God. Deborah could listen to his concerns about the presence of evil and suffering in the world because she could hear without being threatened. However, she hopes to someday be able to say, "Let me show you my God, the God of love."

When I ask whether she misses California, she answers that she misses the ocean but appreciates living where there are rivers and lakes. "At least there's water." She says that she doesn't feel "landlocked." She also misses the fruit, especially the lemons. She describes stuffing her suitcase full of lemons on the return trips to Minnesota after visits to California. As for the Minnesota winters — "Winter is so long! During the summer I forget how long winters are!"

Her adjustment to life in Minnesota was made easier than it might have been because she made "really good friends." She has been able to connect with other African Americans in the Twin Cities. "I built my community from these friendships." She calls her friendships the joy of her life. She adds that being so far from home remains a challenge, that it takes effort to maintain connections and not to lose her community.

Deborah feels blessed by the opportunities that have been open to her. She loves to travel and has made six trips to Europe and three to Africa. "I never thought I'd be an elder in the church, a clerk of session, or a church school teacher."

After her move to Minnesota, Deborah realized that she needed to find a church. When she visited Kwanzaa, she found it to be "friendly, warm, and open." She became part of the church family, and says, "Kwanzaa has fed me ever since."

People come "looking for a church where you are loved." She reports that at Kwanzaa there is "not the classism, the sexism, the pettiness of other churches ... That's the spirit of Kwanzaa ... That's a wonderful thing." She adds that this spirit takes effort to maintain.

"Kwanzaa," she says, "is one of the few places where you can be yourself." According to Deborah, the attitude is, "Come as you are and you will be accepted. You will be loved as you are. You are accepted as you are but loved into being a better person."

Deborah reflects on her own personal and spiritual growth. She says that people tell her they are attracted to her because of the peace they find in her presence. "The older I get, the more I realize that life with God is a journey. The goal is intimacy with God. Developing and maintaining intimacy with God is ongoing. That is the same with any relationship. When you forget that, the relationship falls apart."

She speaks of the challenge "to understand that God uses everyone and that includes me. When we see someone who is living a life that reflects God, we want to ask, 'What makes you like that?' When that person talks about God, it confirms what you are seeing."

In Jesus Deborah finds a model for living and for truth-telling. "A great thing about Jesus was that he could tell people what they needed to hear in a way they could hear if they were open. Jesus was a great model of someone who tells people the truth in love."

Deborah's commitment to truth-telling does not mean settling for easy answers. She describes a conversation between friends who were discussing the question, "Who is Jesus?" Some answered that Jesus is "Lord and Savior." The conversation challenged Deborah to explore the deeper meanings in the words and in her own faith and life. After a time of reflection, she wrote the following: "As my father's daughter, I find myself unable and even unwilling to give that simplistic answer. I feel obligated to expand upon my answer, to attempt to explain, 'Lord and Savior.' … Will that phrase do justice to the complex relationship that I share with God? Does it tell my story? Will they know that when I think of Jesus I think of love, that love is my first thought, not Lord and Savior, but the epitome, the definition, the Incarnation of Love itself."[2]

Speaking the truth in business, passing on truth to the next generation, living the truth — Deborah is a spiritual daughter of Huldah, the ancient prophet. And as a follower of Jesus, she aims to speak the truth in love and in ways that listeners can hear and understand. Thanks be to God for the prophets who speak truth today.

1. H. Adrian Isabelle, Sr., "Power," from Isabelle's Insights.
2. Deborah Isabelle, "Who is Jesus?"

Questions for Reflection and Discussion

- How did Deborah's parents prepare her to be a truth-teller? Who have been truth-tellers for you? Think of a time when hearing a difficult truth helped you make a hard decision.
- Think of a time you had to tell the truth when it would have been easier to be silent.
- What prevents us from hearing hard truths or facing them? If Huldah were here today, what truths would she address?

For Further Exploration

- What pressures could have prevented Huldah from telling the truth about the book that had been discovered? Compare her response with God's call with that of the reluctant prophet, Jonah. (Jonah 1:1–3)
- What pressures tempt us to be silent when truth needs to be told?
- Unlike the accounts of God's call to Isaiah (Isaiah 6:1–8) and to Jeremiah (Jeremiah 1:4–10), the Bible tells us nothing about Huldah's call to be a prophet. How does God call persons today to speak truths that need to be told?
- How do we discern the truth? Perhaps, like Pilate, we avoid the truth. (John 18:37–38) How can we use the Bible in a responsible, informed way to know the truth? (See A Brief Statement of Faith, pp. 52–71; The Westminster Confession of Faith, 6.009.)
- Do you agree with Deborah that, in the United States, we need to have an honest discussion about race? What truths need to be told, remembered, and faced in order for this to take place?

CHAPTER 6

Living Courage: Vashti and Janet

A Letter to Vashti, Esther 1:1–21

Dear Vashti,

Why did you do it? Why did you defy your husband, the king of Persia? When you refused to put your body on display at his banquet, you risked everything: your crown, the honors due to the queen, the hope that one of your sons would be king.

To be sure, your husband didn't sound very bright. Or perhaps after 187 days of feasting, he wasn't thinking very clearly. He didn't seem to realize how inconsistent he was. The law of Persia decreed that his guests — rich or poor, mighty or powerless — could choose whether or not to imbibe. But when he ordered you to appear, most likely unclothed, he didn't give you a choice.

I've always wondered why the king commanded you to come to the party. Was his order some sort of loyalty test? Or perhaps he wanted to exhibit what he, and no other man in the empire, owned. When you disobeyed, he didn't know what to do. So he called in his cabinet. They practically sprang at the king with their demand that he proclaim a new law ordering all women everywhere to honor and obey their husbands.

This leads me to another possibility. Maybe the king's advisors had already been plotting your downfall, and your defiance handed them the perfect opportunity to act. Your threat to their manhood made your demise urgent. If news of your action as a strong woman reached their wives, who knew what might happen when they got home after the party!

The big question was, "Who has the power — power over women's bodies and power over the empire?" Since the king couldn't think or act for himself, the advisors must have seen you as the power behind the throne. I can see it now, conspirators huddled around an oil lamp in the dark of night, plotting to save the kingdom (and their own power, of course). It was all for the good of the empire! (I wonder how they dealt with your successor, Queen Esther. Her only resources were her wits and her sexuality, but she used them well to save her people and to topple the most powerful man in the kingdom.)

I've always wondered, too, what happened to you after you were banished from the king's presence. Many believe that you were Nebuchadnezzar's daughter. If you were, your marriage would have been arranged for political reasons. Your family must have been scandalized by your outrageous behavior. I wonder if they took you back, or if you spent the rest of your life as a prisoner in the king's harem.

Yes, Vashti, you risked everything: your crown, your privileges, and your power. And you lost everything, everything except what was most important — your respect for yourself. That is why we remember you. Throughout the centuries your spiritual daughters have been inspired and empowered by your story. So we will continue to tell your story as long as women are struggling for dignity, self-respect, and wholeness.

Janet's Story

Why does a dream wither and die? What keeps a dream alive? Janet's passion was to write, until racism crushed her hope and silenced her voice. But Janet is a risk-taker; she lives with courage. After many years, she has rediscovered her voice and is living her dream.

In high school her poems and short stories amazed her teachers. They called her the best writer who had ever attended the school. One of her English teachers assigned two short pieces by Lorraine Hannsbery[1] for her to read. The excitement of discovering a Black woman writer and actually reading her works fed Janet's passion to write.

But, in Janet's words, "There were lots of mixed messages in those times." The white teacher who assigned a Black woman writer was the same teacher who "burst her bubble." (Janet says he was trying to be "realistic" and "helpful.") He told her that no one would hire a writer who was a Black girl.

Janet describes the loss of her dream. "I was living in an environment where [risk-taking] wasn't allowed. I was not surrounded by people who wanted me to do more, to broaden my experience. So instead of exploring how it could work, we went straight to 'It can't work.'" She enrolled in an accounting course and set aside her writing.

"During that time I wrote a lot of poetry," she says. "I saved very little of it. I started a few short stories but did not reconnect to writing with any real intention of being a writer until I was in my forties." Her unfinished works, now in storage containers, served as inspiration for the time she would reclaim her dream.

Janet was born in Tampa, and her family moved to Indianapolis when she was two years old. There, the family lived in an all-Black neighborhood. Her school, her teachers, the police — all were Black. She remembers that there was no "crossing the lines." The only white people she saw were downtown. She viewed the world outside her community as unsafe.

When Janet was in seventh grade, she and her friends began to hear about school integration. "The prospect of being taken away from everything we knew and going into areas where Black people didn't feel safe was frightening. We didn't know how severe the white response would be. The grand wizard of the Ku Klux Klan lived in Indiana."

Nevertheless, even before integration became mandatory, Janet volunteered to be one of the students who, in 1970, integrated an all-white high school. When I ask why she made that choice, she says that her elementary school was one of the best Black schools in the city but that she had no assurance that she would get into one of the better Black high schools. She was determined to get a good education, even when she discovered that no transportation was provided, that every day she must take three city buses, beginning at 5:30 a.m., to get to school.

Janet describes the confusion during the first day in the new school. The arriving Black students were all detained in the reception area. The principal's assistant who "greeted" them had no idea what to do. She finally called the principal and asked, "What do I do with them?" The principal's logical response was, "Send them to class." So it was, that forty Black students integrated a large urban high school.

Teachers assumed that the Black students would be far behind academically. However, Janet remembers that her teachers in elementary school had made very sure that their students would do well. Janet and her friends surprised their new teachers by their high performance.

When I ask about the response of the white students, Janet describes three groups: the "super-nice," the "curious," and those who wanted nothing to do with them. By their junior year, Janet and her friends were being invited into the homes of white friends. Nevertheless, the Black students felt a need to go to new places either in groups or escorted by adults in order to feel safe.

69

I ask Janet to reflect on her experience as a Black student in an integrated school. "It was good in some respects. It helped me move on, and I bypassed some of the traps in the poor Black schools: the effects of poverty and the high rate of teen pregnancy." "Moving on" meant her ability to adjust to a major life change — a new home in a new city.

After graduation she moved to Minneapolis to join her family who had recently relocated. She experienced Minneapolis as a more open society where one could get a job because of ability, not because of who you knew. She did not find the rigid social classes she had known in Indianapolis where she remembers stratification in both Black and white communities. "Wherever you were, that's just where you stayed. There was no crossing the line."

In Minneapolis she was also surprised by her younger siblings' freedom. As a child, Janet had always been confined to playing in her own yard. In their new home in Minnesota, her siblings were able not only to leave their own yard but even to explore a nearby park.

Janet was surprised, however, at the small Black population. She remembers going downtown and seeing "no one who looked like me." She compared her experience to a movie in which all Black people disappeared for a day! She remembers feeling "isolated" but not "excluded."

Because their experiences enabled them to gain a different perspective, Janet and her siblings became cultural interpreters for their parents. She compared their experiences to those of immigrant families whose children learn the new language. Janet and her siblings learned to "speak white."

Before she moved, Janet had been taking business courses and, in her words, she "hated them." She says she knew that "There had to be something else." She continued her education at the University of Minnesota. She then joined the corporate world, first working for a bank, then for an insurance company. She was on the way up!

But all was not well in her life. Of her fourteen years in the corporate world, Janet says, "I was managing but not thriving. I didn't know who I was. I was not creating what I was meant to create. I was not honoring the spirit of who I was."

So, like Vashti, Janet took a risk. "My personality is to take risks," she says. Janet left the corporate world. She threw off the expectations others had laid on her. Like Vashti, Janet left a world of security and comfort. It was time to take her first steps toward reclaiming her dream and the life she believed God was planning for her.

After she left the business world, she volunteered at a shelter for people who were homeless. Soon the agency hired her to work weekends and when funding became available, she began working full-time for the organization.

But it was time for Janet to take a giant leap. She started her own nonprofit organization, Life Design Education. She describes the effort as a motivational program, designed to train and support participants for "high impact" change. The unique program required advanced students to work in teams to plan and carry out projects for social service organizations selected by the teams. During the three months' duration of their projects, some teams not only gave their time but also raised significant funds for their organizations.

Janet also worked one-on-one with clients who wanted change in their lives. The first step in what Janet calls her "soft shift" approach was to discover what clients really wanted. The question was, "What do I want to change?" Her approach was very different from what she calls our "microwave society." She believes that people don't take time to set personal goals. "People need to be okay with slow results."

Janet's life changed again when, in 2009, she began work at Kwanzaa as the church administrator. At that time she was working with a new business model but had to close Life Design Education and discontinue her motivational counseling because of the time required by her new position. She discovered that church work is not an eight-to-five job, because most working people call her in the evening.

Even though Janet was working a more-than-fulltime job, her dream, deferred but never dead, led her to take her biggest risk: reclaiming her identity as a writer. When I ask how she began to write again, she answers, "I started to journal and my voice started to come back. Some forms started to come, and I felt comfortable going back to writing. I had begun to understand God's blessings in my life, so I knew the story would come. It would just take time for it to develop."

Her world had expanded since her youthful time as a writer. "When I understood that I could write, I wasn't sure what I wanted to say. I wasn't on the same path." Her writing needed to reflect where she was in her own personal journey.

As Janet has rediscovered her voice, the story and the words have come. Reflecting on her relationship with her mother, Janet began the first of two books, *Message From Discord*. At the time of our last interview she said, "I'll be working on this till the end of my life."

Sharing her thoughts on a second book, *Explaining Air*, she says, "We look for ways to explain God, and there are some things we just don't have the ability to explain. It's about the experience. I can describe what [air], but I was breathing long before I could describe it. So the experience was with me whether I figured it out or not. I believe God is with us in the same way. It's nice if we can come up with a packaged idea of who God is, but the experience is with us while we are learning."

Explaining Air has been reborn as part of a brave new venture. Janet is using poetry and prose to integrate her reflections into *Light Topics*, a website on women's spiritual expressions. She is collecting women's stories that present spiritual viewpoints and women's spiritual awakenings. "Readers will see what others have experienced, what others have learned, and will have the opportunity to express their own ideas and see the ideas of others. The website will invite women to express themselves and allow others to add their own experiences."

Talking with Janet, my imagination takes me back many centuries to the court of King Ahasuerus, where Queen Vashti surrendered comfort and security for her personhood. Decades later, like the ancient queen of Persia, Janet left security behind to dare a giant leap into an uncertain future. We grieve for the many women who, like Vashti, have suffered for the risks they have taken and the courage they have shown. But we are grateful that one risk-taker, Janet, has sought and rediscovered her own voice and the stories she needs to tell — her own and those of other women. "I've seen God work in my life," she says. To this we can say, "Thanks be to God!"

1. In Lorraine Hansberry's play *A Raisin in the Sun,* the characters struggle to fulfill their dreams in spite of the oppression they face as African Americans. The title comes from Langston Hughes' famous poem about a lost dream that shrivels "like a raisin in the sun." Zora Neale Hurston's groundbreaking book, *Their Eyes Were Watching God,* was published in 1937.

Questions for Reflection and Discussion

- Think about a time in your life (or in the life of someone you know well) when you had to take a risk in order to do what you believed to be right or in order to fulfill a dream.
- When we are called to take great risks, what are the obstacles and where can we find strength and support?
- How is Jesus a model and guide for those who are called upon to act with great courage?

For Further Exploration

- Name a dreamer whose vision and courage won freedom for her or his people.
- What obstacles prevent young African Americans today from fulfilling their dreams? What part do generational poverty and racism play?
- How has the African-American church supported the dreams of young women and men?

CHAPTER 7

Living Purpose: Esther and Ruby

Esther's Story, Esther 25:1

I am the queen of Persia, but I am breaking the law of the land. I am walking, uninvited, into the inner court of my husband, the king. If King Ahasuerus holds out his golden scepter to me, I shall live. If he does not, I shall die. Queen Vashti lost her crown; I may lose my life. But I have made my choice.

But what choice did I have? What will my life be if my people, the Jews, are annihilated? The words of my cousin Mordecai are still ringing in my ears. I cannot stop them. "Perhaps you have come to royal dignity for just such a time as this."

When Queen Vashti refused to put her body on display, I was still a young girl. I was an orphan, being raised by Mordecai. We lived here in Susa, the capital of the empire, but like all the Jews in Persia, we are exiles. We are far from our homes in Jerusalem.

I became the queen because after the king banned Vashti, he ordered his officers to every corner of the kingdom. He commanded them to gather all the beautiful virgins for his harem. Wailing rose throughout the empire as soldiers tore girls from their mothers' arms. Fathers wept when they could not protect their daughters.

When the officers invaded our community, Mordecai rushed me into the closet. It was unthinkable for a Jew to marry a heathen king. Many families hid their daughters, so many that the king decreed that any girl who tried to escape would be put to death.[1]

There was no escape for me. My screams, my tears, my struggles to flee the soldiers could not save me. In the harem the sweet-smelling oils and the spices that made my skin glow and my hair shine were no balm for my loneliness.

As for Mordecai, every day he paced back and forth in front of the harem, always seeking news about me. He is a lowly official in the royal court, but did he, even then, suspect the gathering storm? Was he, even then, hearing whispers of doom for our people? The palace reeks of intrigue.

After a year of beauty treatments, I was presented to the king. He "loved" me, and I was crowned queen with all the splendor, all the pomp of the empire. But even as my husband placed the gold crown, heavy with jewels, on my head, I remembered Vashti. She kept her dignity. I shuddered, wondering what choices might be forced upon me.

The king does not know that I am a Jew. Sometimes at night when all is quiet except for the beating of my heart, a small voice whispers, taunting me: "What if the king discovers who you are?"

My foreboding proved true. Jealousy, lust for power, even the threat of assassination stalked every chamber, every hall in the palace. Outside the walls, evil, like an angry beast was lurking, ready to spring.

Haman, an official in the royal court, had risen to become the king's closest advisor. The king decreed that whenever Haman passed, all the people must bow low to honor him. Only Mordecai refused.

Haman raged, but his threats did not move Mordecai. So Haman went to the king and accused the Jews, all the Jews, of flouting the laws of the empire. To the king, this was high treason. So the king sent messengers far and wide, to every village and city in the kingdom, to announce that on a day he had set, his soldiers will kill every Jew, even the children, and plunder everything they own.

But the palace walls have ears, and soon Mordecai heard the news. As Jews do when they are mourning, he tore his clothes, sat in ashes, and wailed. All of Susa heard his terrible howling. Not understanding, I sent him new clothes — much finer than the ones he had shredded. He refused them. Instead, he sent me a message with the news of the king's outrage.

I was struck dumb with disbelief. It could not be true! I tried to tell myself that it could not be. Even the king would not issue so monstrous an order. But I knew my husband's anger. In my heart I knew it was true.

But there was more in Mordecai's message. He begged me to go to the king and plead for the lives of our people. But what could I do? I felt powerless. How could my cousin, who was like a father to me, ask such a thing? He was asking me to risk, even sacrifice, my life. Surely, if I went to the king, he would suspect that I, too, am a Jew. Besides, the law was clear.

I sent my answer to Mordecai: "All the servants and all the people of the king's provinces know that if any man or woman goes to the king inside the inner court without being called, there is but one law —

all alike are to be put to death. Only if the king holds out the golden scepter to someone, may that person live."

Mordecai did not yield. "Do not think that in the king's palace you will escape any more than all of the other Jews. For if you keep silence at such a time as this, relief and deliverance will rise for the Jews from another quarter, but your father's family will perish. Who knows? Perhaps you have come to royal dignity for just such a time as this."

I made my choice. (Did I really have a choice?) I sent word to Mordecai, "I will go to the king …. and if I perish, I perish." I asked all the Jews in Susa to hold a three-day fast for me. My maids and I did the same.

So now I am standing at the marble entrance to the inner court. The guards are confused; they don't know what to do. They must know I've not been summoned by the king. Nevertheless, until I must bow low before my husband, I will hold my head high. I am wearing the robes that befit my station — the queen's purple. The diamonds that circle my veil, my ruby and emerald bracelets — all reflect the brilliance of the sunlight that I pray I shall live to see tomorrow.

I am beautiful but I have more than a pretty face and a sensual body. I have a plan. I understand the intrigue of the palace. If I live, I shall reveal my true identity as a Jew and I shall expose Haman.

I don't know what awaits me on the other side of the door. But I pray that someday the daughters of Vashti and the daughters of my people will remember that we walked with dignity, standing straight and tall. We confronted imperial power with courage, with strength, with integrity. Perhaps Mordecai was right; I have come to the royal court "for such a time as this."

1. The story of Mordecai hiding Esther was told by the ancient rabbis and is quoted by Lewis Bayles Paton in the *Book of Esther*, p. 173. The International Critical Commentary. New York: Charles Scribner's Sons; 1908. (Cited by Katheryn Pfisterer Darr, *Far More Precious than Gold*, pp. 172–173.)

Ruby's Story

Ruby does not hesitate when I ask her to name a biblical woman with whom she identifies. "Esther! I'm here for a purpose," she says. She believes that through the many choices and challenges of her life, she has been where she was needed to be "for such a time as this."

After graduating from cosmetology school in Evanston, Indiana, in 1981, Ruby was looking forward to a promising career. She saw herself on the road to success.

Then her life took an unexpected turn. Her twenty-three-year old sister died suddenly of a rare disease. Her death left three sons with no parent to care for them. Tawara was six, Tyshawn was four, and Tareace was two. Ruby and her mother took responsibility for the boys.

A year and a half later, Ruby moved to Minneapolis to pursue a new career opportunity. She joined a big salon whose owner hoped to break into the ethnic market. Ruby was the only Black hair stylist. She left after three years because she saw no way to advance.

She moved on to a new salon. Soon she was doing the hair for the owner who recognized her talent. This was her chance; she broke into management. She supervised three salons until, after six years, it was time to go independent. She was ready to open her own salon.

In the meantime, while she was building her career, Ruby was living with her good friend Peggy (see "Living Advocacy: The Syro-Phoenician Woman and Peggy") and her remaining sister, Rhonda. After three years Ruby's mother and the three boys joined them in Minnesota. Then Ruby's life turned again.

At the height of her career, when she was thirty, Ruby became an "instant mom." Her mother died, leaving the three boys who were then in third, fifth, and seventh grades. Like Esther, it seemed that Ruby had been born "for such a time as this."

Ruby waited until 1996, when the boys were out of high school to open her own salon. It had taken a long time, but finally, on December 31, 1996, her dreams became a reality.

Eight months later, Ruby again became a primary caregiver, this time for Tareace's nine-month-old son, Charlie. His eighteen-year-old mother was unable to care for him. Ruby's home welcomed both Tareace and Charlie.

According to his proud grandmother, Charlie, who was fourteen at the time of this interview, is "a fabulous young man with a bright future." He is majoring in musical theater at the St. Paul Conservatory for Performing Artists. Ruby says that he is so goal-oriented, he began to research high schools when he was a seventh grader. "He never wavered. He knew he wanted to act when he was in kindergarten and first grade. There is something special about Charlie. He is conscious of other people's feelings."

When Tareace was "caught up in street activities," Ruby faced a new challenge. Her youngest son is now serving a twenty-year sentence in a maximum-security prison. Speaking of the demands upon her, she says, "You can never stop parenting, even in prison."

She shared some of her thoughts about Tareace's imprisonment and their relationship. "I can always tell when he's depressed or when he is in trouble. He'll call and say he's tired of the people, tired of the atmosphere. He'll tell me, 'I just need a hug.' At thirty-two he's still my baby."

Ruby and Charlie visit Tareace every Sunday afternoon. Describing her feelings as doors are being locked behind them and as they are being searched, she says, "When you go into prison, you drop your own freedom." However, she describes the prison staff as "respectful." Sometimes they say wonderful things about Tareace. "That always makes me feel good."

Ruby is concerned about Tareace's future. She is encouraging him to take college courses so that he will be able to work when he is released. "I try to have him see his importance as a man of our family."

Ruby says that she cannot be critical of parents who cannot maintain a relationship with a son who is in prison. She describes the relationship as "not easy … Sometimes I just have to go in and tell him off … It's a commitment. It doesn't suit everyone." However, Ruby calls her relationship with Tareace "another form of giving love." She says, "His mental and spiritual freedom depends on me."

Ruby's relationship with Tareace is a challenge, but her grandchildren are her joy. "When they call me Nana, it makes life worth living. They think I'm a rock star." She loves to gather all of them together for hot dogs and sidewalk art. At "Nana" gatherings, the neighbors know the children are there because their art covers the entire block. "It makes me feel important."

Speaking of her grandchildren, she says, "I want my grandchildren to know who they are and whose they are. I want them to know they can get through anything with Christ in their lives. That's the way it was for me."

In a life marked by challenges, another struck on May 22, 2011, when a tornado ripped through north Minneapolis, damaging most of the homes in Ruby's neighborhood. Two ninety-foot evergreens fell on her house. Three weeks passed before they could be removed, and five months passed before repair work could begin on her house. The community rallied in support, and many wanted to help but did not have the necessary equipment. One who offered assistance was a young man, of whom she says, "We'll be friends for life."

She reflects that only her patience and her faith saw her through those months, "When I really let go and got out of the way, things began to happen." She believes that she got her house "through God" and that her home was never just for herself. "I've lived alone for only six months in my whole life."

At Kwanzaa Ruby is "Deacon Ruby," and like all the deacons at Kwanzaa, she has her "deacon family." Pastor Ralph calls her Deacon of the World. Ruby says that she tries to live up to his praise.

She knows that God called her to Kwanzaa. Yet she says that she joined "in spite of myself." She admits that for her, "Everything had to be grand." The church was not yet chartered when she began to attend with the handful of others who were beginning to gather for worship. She couldn't see where she would fit in. But she heard "a message I didn't want to hear." She believes that God was telling her, "This is the place. Join!" Ruby may have been reluctant to join Kwanzaa, but she says, "As Kwanzaa has grown, I've also grown."

Ruby is considering attending seminary but is quick to say that she does not want to preach. "After thirty years as a hair stylist, my ministry is listening." She expresses fascination about life in the time of Jesus: "As I grow spiritually, my desire is to know more about how Christianity has grown."

Looking back on her life, Ruby says that her ability to achieve some of her goals, both professional and personal, has "amazed me." She is a world traveler. "I have seen some things I never thought this little Black girl from Indiana would see." She has toured Holland, Italy, and Portugal. She has not yet visited Africa, but she is looking forward to doing so someday. For right now, her most important goal is "to get Charlie where he needs to be."

The choices have not always been easy for a professional woman who has raised three sons and is now raising a teenager. Ruby has had to "make choices to go in one way or another." She says, " I could have taken another road that would have forced me to disconnect from my family." But she says she has "no regrets." To Ruby the love of her family "means more than any amount of money."

Speaking of her family, Ruby says, "The balance between my professional life and the needs of the children is always a part of making decisions. I need to be here. I need to be at my best. My goal is to teach them to live as righteous lives as they can." She asserts that she never felt forced to be a caregiver. "It was not just for them, but for me."

Her own childhood offered a model of caring. She recalls that she was one of thirty-two grandchildren. The adults and children talked about their lives around the table. "If a child got a bad grade at school, the adults asked, 'Why did you get that bad grade?' That tradition was passed on to me. Caring for my family never felt like a burden. Our lives are not just about us." She has passed on the model of caring to her sons. She describes Tawara and Tyshawn as "fabulous, hands-on daddies."

Others may wonder where Ruby finds her strength. Ruby's answer is, "Believing in God and what God sees in you, seeing yourself as Jesus sees you ... to love myself as I believe Jesus does. Jesus gives us a push and encourages us. The end game is to see Jesus face to face."

Ruby describes her life as an adventure, a journey, on which she is "open to joy." She says that through the twists and turns of the journey she looks to Jesus as her constant companion. Her faith enables her to "embrace the journey." She sums up her life by saying, "God has blessed me to be a blessing." We might add, "for such a time as this."

Questions for Reflection and Discussion

- Why do you think Esther chose to go to the king even though it meant risking her life?
- Has there been a time in your life when you felt called to act "for such a time as this"? What did you risk? What gave you strength and courage?
- What difference does it make in your life if you have a strong sense of purpose?

For Further Exploration

- In what ways is Esther a spiritual ancestor for Ruby?
- Tell the story of a woman (either historic or modern) who took a great risk to serve or to save her people.
- Try to step inside the stories of these biblical women. How did a sense of purpose influence their actions or the lives of others?
    - ❑ The daughters of Zelophehad (Numbers 27:1–8)
    - ❑ Ruth (Ruth 1:1–18)
    - ❑ Anna (Luke 2:36–38)
    - ❑ The women at the tomb (Luke 23:55–56, 24:1–12)

CHAPTER 8

Living in the Wider World: the Hemorrhaging Woman, Alanna, Holley, and Caroline

The Woman's Story, Mark 5:25–34

I knew I was breaking our sacred law, but what choice did I have? I had been bleeding for twelve years. I was desperate.

Long ago before my illness, I was a rich woman. I had a large house where I loved to entertain guests. I served the finest wine, bread made of finely sifted whole wheat flour and olive oil, and the most succulent lamb in our village. When our people celebrated, none of the women loved to sing and dance more than I did.

Everything changed when my bleeding started and would not stop. Our holy law, the law passed down through many generations of our people, called me unclean … impure. No one was allowed to touch me. No one was allowed to touch my bed or even a chair where I had sat. On our holy days I could not celebrate with my people. I was an outcast.

The stories of our people teach that God called the Jews to be a holy people, holy like God is holy. Anyone who has leprosy, anyone who touches a dead body, or a woman who is having her monthly period is unclean. When we are unclean, we are cut off from our people until we are cleansed. There could be no cleansing for me.

I tried everything. I spent all I had on doctors who promised they could cure me. They gave me their potions. One sent me to find a barleycorn in the dung of a she-ass. I was desperate enough to try even that. Nothing helped, and there was nothing more I could try. My wealth was gone, and my hope was dying like a vine cursed by the desert sun.

But hope — hope I was afraid to feel — began to sprout again like tiny green shoots when travelers passed through our village with stories of a healer named Jesus. One told that he had been blind before Jesus gave him his sight. Another came with his son who, he said, had been near death with a fever until Jesus cured him. The townspeople marveled as they watched the boy running and playing with the village boys.

I told myself, "Careful — don't hope. Even if Jesus comes to our town, how can you go to him? You are unclean — untouchable." Besides, it is not right for any woman to approach a man in public, especially if he is a rabbi. I had no man to plead for me.

I have always been a bit of a rebel. When I was a child, my parents thought I was disobedient because I wanted to run with my brothers instead of working with the women. Perhaps I am still a rebel because I knew, even as I argued with myself, that I would go to Jesus!

I didn't have long to wait. Early one morning, our town began to buzz with excitement. Jesus was on his way! The news spread as women filled water jugs at the town well and as the men mended fishing nets together. Soon the town was nearly deserted as both the miracle-seekers and the curious rushed to be the first to see Jesus.

The road was alive with the gathering crowd when a runner approached with another story. Jesus was on his way to the house of Jairus, the ruler of the synagogue. Jairus' daughter was said to be near death. I could feel my hope withering. Who could interrupt the healer on his way to Jairus' house? Jairus was an important man. He could not be kept waiting. All my fears and all my doubts tormented me like angry demons. I could almost hear them laughing at me: "Who are you? You are nobody but an unclean woman ... untouchable!"

Nevertheless, I could not stay away. I followed the crowd. At first I kept my distance but before long, I too had joined the jostling throng. I gathered my tattered veil around my face, hoping no one would recognize me.

Keeping my head low, I pushed my way through the crowd until I was right behind Jesus. I saw the tassels at the corners of his garment, the tassels that show that a man is a devout Jew. Then the truth struck me. I knew that I was more than an unclean woman. I too am a Jew; I am a daughter of Abraham! I told myself, "If I can but touch his clothes, I will be made well." I stooped low, reached out, and touched the cloak of the healer.

It was only a touch but I felt the power of the healer. My bleeding stopped. I wanted to shout, to run, to touch my friends, my neighbors, my brothers, my sisters.

There was something more I must do. I must purify myself, then take my offering to the priest. But a firm voice stopped me. The words, "Who touched my clothes?" rang above the shouts and cries of the crowd. I was close enough to hear a muffled growl, "You can see the crowd, how can you say, 'Who touched me?'"

Stunned, I struggled to gather my thoughts: "Should I run? Would it be better to slip away and hope that no one sees me? Should I be quiet and pretend I was not the one?"

But I knew I could not hide. Surely Jesus, whoever he was, was sent by God, and I could not escape God's eye. But maybe — maybe the healer God sent would be merciful. I knew what I had to do.

I was trembling so hard I feared I could not move but I threw myself at his feet. I told him the story of my humiliation. Off to the side, through a corner of my eye, I could see a man motioning to Jesus to hurry.

Jesus was in no hurry. At that moment I knew that he saw no one but me. "Daughter, your faith has made you well; go in peace and be healed of your disease."

So I am cured of my disease, but my life is also healed. I am whole. I am restored to my family, my community, and my people. I am at peace. Thanks be to God!

Alanna's Story

Faith, *courage*, and *imagination*: Alanna uses these three words to describe the woman with the hemorrhage. "She could still imagine a life that was whole." She goes on to reflect, "The woman did such a little thing. What is the little thing that can be a big way to express oneself?" Some of the experiences in Alanna's life may have seemed "small" at the time, but together, they have led her into a wider world of personal and professional development.

Alanna grew up in Chicago's South Side with three older sisters and two younger brothers. She jokingly describes her youngest sibling as an "outsider" because she was seventeen when he was born. Along with Alanna's parents and siblings, the other important person in their home was her grandmother. Alanna and her grandmother shared one of the three bedrooms in their home, so Alanna feels that she received "lots of special attention" from her grandmother. She was able to watch her grandmother's life "close up." Alanna calls this relationship "a wonderful experience."

Alanna describes her parents as "very supportive." Her father was creative and handy, and took pride in their well-kept home. Education was important to the parents; Alanna's mother was always in touch with the children's schools. "She always knew what was happening." Alanna remembers that her mother expected an increasing level of responsibility from her as she grew.

Alanna recalls the community where her family lived as "an ideal place to be." The residents were hard-working, with intact families. She felt secure because there was "a real sense of community." She knew that she was "known and loved by lots of adults."

High school was an "adventure." Alanna's elementary school, which she describes as "great," had been within walking distance from her home. Getting to high school, however, required taking three buses. Admission to the all-city school was based on entrance exams. Its mission was to prepare students for college. School was "hard and good." Alanna discovered that there are "a lot of smart people in the world."

Alanna says that the teachers "drove us." Older students at her high school, some of whom were from her church, set high standards. Alanna, however, met or exceeded those challenges and was always in the high academic track. Besides getting good grades, she was active in the drama club, the United Nations club, and Future Business Leaders of America.

Along with academic excellence, Alanna's high school had good counselors who helped students figure out their college applications. Alanna remembers being met by a counselor in the hallway who told her that she did not have her college application. "Do you want me to call your mother?" she asked. That was all Alanna needed to get started!

Through academic and personal challenges, Alanna's world was expanding. Her family's neighborhood was all African American, as was her elementary school. She recalls that her all-Black grade school seemed "just natural." Her high school was more diverse. It included about twenty percent Asian Americans and a few white students. Of her high school years, she says, "I grew into my own sense of making my way in the world." Reflecting on her experience, she says, "God has blessed me." She believes that she was being led into "a little bigger pond."

Alanna describes "the amazing place church had in my life." She credits Trinity United Church of Christ (UCC) as playing a central role in her development. According to Alanna, much of the focus of mission at Trinity was, "What does it mean to be both African American and a Christian?"

Trinity Church was committed to providing strong leadership for its children and youth. Alanna and her siblings attended the equivalent of Sunday School on Saturday mornings. She remembers having wonderful Saturday School teachers, some of whom were outstanding professionals. The church welcomed and included both professional and blue-collar workers but, as is true in the culture of the Black church, everyone was equal. There were no class distinctions. Alanna describes her teachers and mentors as "amazing people who wanted those [good] experiences for the kids."

As Alanna found her horizons growing broader, the church offered her the opportunity to learn leadership skills. As a teenager she was active in the United Church of Christ at the local, state, and national level. Twice she served as a youth delegate to the General Synod, the church-wide denominational gathering. She also remembers her "godfather" taking six teenage girls, including herself, to denominational policy meetings for discussion of issues such as divestment.

Trinity's effort to "be faithful to what God has entrusted to us" included a serious commitment to the world. "The church kept me mindful of how big the world was," Alanna says. She remembers a big sign on the church, Free South Africa. Church members held discussions on world affairs and engaged in critiques of politics and society as a follow-up to the Civil Rights era. Trinity members did more than talk; they offered practical help to people who needed it. There were monthly collections of food and, while Alanna was a Trinity member, the church opened a day-care center for children.

Alanna is convinced that without the church, "My world would have been a lot smaller." Travel experiences offered by the church enriched her widening world and her personal growth. She says that she has actually asked a friend who shared her experiences at Trinity, "Did we really get to grow up the way we think we did?"

Alanna spent her four college years at Grinnell College, which she describes as "a small school with a big perspective." Reflecting on her college years, she says, "I would like to have had six years to find myself." According to Alanna, she "fell in love with Grinnell" after visiting the campus as part of a summer program during her high school years. She admits, however, that it took some convincing for her parents to let her apply at Grinnell.

Of her experience at Grinnell, Alanna says, "God worked it out." In some ways being on her own at Grinnell was "a sobering experience," but she names two people with connections to her

Chicago community who "were looking out for me." They were the interim chaplain, who had been an intern at Trinity UCC, and a staff member in the administration office whose mother knew Alanna's mother. She says, "I first recognized my minority status at Grinnell," but goes on to add, "I found lots of people I had a lot in common with." She recalls making good friends with students from a variety of backgrounds, especially the international students.

Her life took an important turn when she found a new direction for her future. "I really liked policy and political science." She graduated from Grinnell with a major in political science.

After college Alanna worked as an intern for Minnesota's legislative audit bureau. She recalls being attracted to Minnesota because of its reputation for good government. She says she loved studying issues and passing on her research to the policy makers.

From her internship in Minnesota, she moved on to a similar full-time position in a state office in Wisconsin. In her first "real job" for the State of Wisconsin, she became an analyst, evaluating markets for recyclable products. Another of her assignments was to study school integration in order to determine whether bussing was working. Alanna's contribution to this project was leading statewide focus groups for youth. She "loved it."

At times she was the object of racial slurs, but she says, "I could handle it because of my experience." She explains, "You know your own abilities. You need to say what needs to be said." Quoting from Luke 12:48, she continues, "From everyone to whom much has been given, much will be required; and from the one to whom much has been entrusted, even more will be demanded." Remembering her own experience growing up in the church, she says, "Parents need to pick a church like Trinity if you are trying to raise children with a sense of responsibility to others."

After about two years, Macalester College lured her back to Minnesota, where she accepted a position in the multicultural affairs office. A goal of the multicultural program was to help minority students feel welcome and comfortable at the prestigious college. In order to do so, it was necessary to have an impact on all students and to link the multicultural and academic disciplines. Alanna used her analytical background to draw upon and spotlight academic research on the relationship between multiculturalism and other fields. Her work also involved relationship building: helping students from different minority groups relate to one another and encouraging minority students to develop relationships with faculty members.

Alanna describes some of her favorite projects. She recalls the passionate presentation given by an African-American student who had gone to Ghana to study drum making. Alanna herself was responsible for the office of multicultural affairs's mentoring program, and she was an advisor to the multicultural student organizations. She and Reverend Lucy Forster-Smith worked together to bring multiculturalism into the chapel. One example was a chapel observance of the Mexican Day of the Dead.

In 1998 she accepted a position at Hennepin County, Minnesota's most populous county. Beginning as an analyst in the economic assistance unit, in 2002 she moved to county administration, where she "got to see everything that was part of county government."

One of the advantages in her position was finding a mentor. She describes him as asking "brilliant questions." She was able to discuss career issues with him and, in doing so, she realized that she needed to gain experience managing people. She needed to learn and practice public leadership. Thinking as a person of faith she asked herself, "What might God be up to?"

Her work in administration has given her many opportunities to practice public leadership. This included managing the county's purchasing, anything not related to human services. Her new position offered new challenges. One of these was the need to learn conflict resolution. When she was confronted by difficult problems, she discovered, "I don't get to not be a Christian at work"

Speaking of her life in Minnesota, Alanna says, "This is where I came into my own." She doesn't get lonely easily because she has "tremendous relationships" with whom she shares her interests in food and walking. She feels blessed to have friends through church, "friends who are like family."

When Alanna enrolled at Luther Seminary in St. Paul, she faced a new challenge: balancing school with a demanding professional life. She recalls a time, shortly after she started her current job when, within a single month, she was preaching at Kwanzaa, going to school, and dealing with a very difficult personnel problem at work. At that time she had to remind herself, "God has this thing figured out."

Alanna's decision to go to seminary was not sudden. As long ago as her sophomore year in high school she knew that ministry was on her horizon. She is thankful for the life experiences she has had: "I'm glad I went to seminary at this point." She believes that her professional experience and her seminary training may enable her to be bi-vocational.

Alanna began the process of searching for her vocation by speaking to her pastor and the all-male board of deacons at the Baptist church she attended from 1991 until 1998. She was required to preach a "trial sermon." She practiced by giving the sermon to her neighbors. Still in her late twenties, she was so nervous that she "cried the whole way through." Nevertheless, after preaching to the congregation, she was licensed by the deacons to preach. She stayed at that congregation, where she led youth groups, until she discovered Kwanzaa.

Alanna's interest in Kwanzaa was piqued by an article about Reverend Alika Galloway in the *Women's Press*. She laughed as she recalls driving around in a circle trying to find the church the first time she attended. But she liked what she saw, and says, "I knew I was ending my membership in St. Paul." She says that other churches had not been what she was looking for. She liked seeing church members sharing in the service and was impressed by the presence of women in leadership. She joined Kwanzaa shortly before the church was chartered in 2002. Then in 2005 she "ran out of reasons not to go to seminary."

As a seminary graduate, what are Alanna's dreams for her ministry? She quips that she hopes "not to get into too much trouble." On a more serious note, she says that she is looking forward to a "great experience."

Alanna speaks about the public Christian leadership approach she hopes to develop. She wants to be a leader "with others leading with me." She does not want to be in a pastor-centric church; she wants the people "to know that the church is theirs." She does not want "the pulpit to keep me apart from the people."

Alanna speaks of her wish for the church to be relevant, for the church to carry on traditions that are familiar but fresh. On the other hand, Alanna hopes to use her skills as an analyst asking, "How do we get to outcomes, measuring inputs and outputs?" She asks, "Why can't we use our skills at church?"

Returning to her long-term personal and professional goals, she raises the possibility of serving the church as a pastor whose primary responsibility is to work for social justice through community organizing. She also shares her response during a recent Presbytery meeting. After listening to a report by the executive presbyter, she thought, "That could be a cool job!"

The three words Alanna used to describe the woman who dared to touch Jesus also catch Alanna's spirit. Her faith was nurtured in home and church; her courage led her to step forward and develop her gifts; her imagination helped her to embrace a wider world. In reflecting on the story of the hemorrhaging woman, she asks, "What is the little thing that can be a big way to express oneself?" We can look forward and affirm the "little things" that will open up the ever-widening horizon for Alanna's life and ministry.

Holley's Story

Out of her comfort zone, risking, trusting — like the woman who pushed through the crowd to touch Jesus, Holley says, "I'm reaching for Jesus."

Holley has lived the journey into the wider world. But the path has twisted and turned, sometimes winding into a maze. "I was lost for so many years," she says. "I had to identify who I was."

Now, reveling in her new world and her new life, she has a job where she feels "so at home and at peace." She has a sense of who she is with a name she has reclaimed as her own. "I was lost but now am found."

Holley was married for fourteen years and separated for six more before she and her husband divorced. She describes herself during those years as "lost in my marriage and lost in my son. I have a son who was abandoned by his father. That led him to a road of destruction."

Her older son lives with attention deficit hyperactivity disorder (ADHD), yet his elementary school failed to give him the support he needed. When he graduated from sixth grade, the principal recommended a military school that was part of the public school system. There, he did well and raised his test scores to grade level. High school was a different story. He started "acting up" and was often truant. Holley met with his teachers and the principal every Friday for eight months. Because he was truant so often, he wore an ankle bracelet that signaled whenever he skipped school. In spite of all Holley and the school could do, he dropped out shortly before graduation.

His problems compounded, and during the next few years, he served several prison terms. At times Holley was able to say, "God is waking him up. I have faith that this is what he needs." At other times she asked, "How can a son of mine be like this?" Despite the pain in their relationship, Holley knew that she was always a presence in his life.

At the time of our last interview, Holley's son had been out of prison for three years. When he was released, it was with a diagnosis of mental illness. Holley describes him as "showing growth in maturity but struggling."[1] Nevertheless, he was working and training for a management position in a fast-food chain.

Holley has been present to her younger son in a different way. He lives in California because "he can't deal with Minnesota winters." His diagnosis of cancer several years ago sent Holley to her church family for support and prayer. He is now cancer free, has graduated from high school, and is working. He is, Holley hopes, headed for college.

Holley knew her "dark night of the soul" while she was struggling to find her own identity as she was doing her best to be present to two sons. She reached the point of giving up, even resigning her responsibilities as a deacon at Kwanzaa. But Pastor Alika told her, in words Holley says she will never forget, "Don't give up. Stay strong. Stay faithful. God has got you."

And Holley did not give up. As a parent who faced extraordinary challenges, she still believes that children are gifts from God. She could never have foreseen that she herself would become a gift for children and a loving presence in many young lives.

Holley believes that her parenting experience and her past jobs all prepared her for her wider world. After working in banking and accounting for many years, she worked for a temp agency during the six years when she was separated from her husband. Her last position required her to sit at a computer all day. One day her supervisor stunned her with the news that her contract job would end in two months. She told her that she could apply for the permanent position but that she needed to be working with people "out in the world."

Holley knew that her supervisor was right, but being "right" would not find her a job in a tight market. Then, as if on cue, the executive director of Patchwork Quilt,[2] where Holley had worked as a temp, sought her out. A full-time permanent position was waiting for her.

Her new world was opening before her with a job that was more than a job — it was a calling.

Holley says, "God prepared me for this through all the jobs I've had. God says, 'I am the potter. You are the clay.' I feel like God molded me into this job. I find myself thanking God every day for putting me in this position."

Holley is the administrative assistant to the executive director of Patchwork Quilt, an after-school program for children who are at risk. Every Monday through Friday forty-five scholars in grades one through six are bussed from their elementary schools to the center. At Patchwork Quilt the scholars read, do math, study Black history, and learn good manners. Volunteers assist with homework.

This is the "official" curriculum, but the unwritten curriculum is love: "We are teaching our scholars to show love. We're teaching them to respect others, to respect themselves.

"I'm an administrator but still have those 'mother's ears.' When they're acting out, it's not because they hate you. A child might have had a bad night, or be hungry, or have to wear the same clothes everyday. The family might be living in a car. You don't know what these children are going through. I tell our volunteers, 'Don't be mad at them. Show them love.'

"I believe that children are the beginning. We teach the children manners and hope that they can teach their parents, 'Please, thank you, I love you.' Or they can go home and tell their parents about Frederick Douglas."

One of Holley's joys is working with volunteers and organizing training sessions. She solves problems like the one brought by a volunteer who admitted, "I can't pronounce their names." At a recent training session, volunteers affirmed her interpersonal and organizational skills by saying, "You are doing a fantastic job. You are so organized." Then they all clapped.

Holley's job has not lacked surprises. Soon after she started, she discovered that she was in charge while her director took several months off to care for a sick daughter. Holley had to use every skill she had learned in her earlier jobs, her gift of organizing, and her gifts for working with people. Administering a program, getting the program licensed, and writing grants pushed her beyond her comfort zone. Nevertheless, she knew that she was in the right place, that this was where God wanted her to be.

Reflecting on her work, she says, "Who would have thought I'd be doing something like this? I never would have thought in a million years that I would be working with children. I never thought I'd be practically running a program, a school for kids.

"My boss sends me to meetings: the Carlson Foundation, Youth Pride, the Science Museum. I even get to go to NAZ meetings. I look around at all those important people and think, 'Here I am.'"

A wider world calls for bigger dreams. Holley shares some of her dreams for her future. Before she began working at Patchwork Quilt, she had considered going to school to study event panning. "I still have three business plans on my computer." School is still a possibility as she has what she calls "many little certificates" but no college. At the time of this interview, she was taking a course, Quality Learning, at the University of Minnesota.

Dreams that were once unreachable are now possible in her wider world. One is to be the director of her own school. But a soon-to-be fulfilled goal is to work as a parent advocate. She explains the role of the parent advocate as being with parents as they meet with teachers, social workers, counselors, doctors — all the professionals in their children's support network.

"I think God was molding me for this. We all know it starts at home. It's up to the parents to fight for their kids and I want to fight for their kids with them. That's my goal."

Holly remembers that finding the way through the maze of services for children can be a bewildering, frustrating experience for parents. "Often the parent doesn't know where to go. I experienced that with my older son. That's why it's really important for me to build these relationships with parents and scholars. I've been through it so I know what it's like."

We do not know the name of the spiritual ancestor who pushed through the crowd to touch Jesus. She is unknown, but not to God. But we can celebrate a new name with Holley, a sign of her new life. As part of claiming her new identity, she reclaimed the name she had before her marriage.

At times it would have been so easy to give up. "It's so scary when change comes. But now I can welcome change. I'm not afraid because change is good. God is with me through all the changes.

"There's a lesson in everything, the bad and the good. I've learned to listen and learn through my experiences, through the changes. I've learned that I don't have to depend on me. I've got somebody that has my back, twenty-four–seven.

"All I have to do is love, honor, give glory and let God lead me. 'Be still and know what I have for you.' I believe that's what all those years were about. I know that God was with me the whole time."

In her new life, Holley continues to reach, touch, and trust, "I'm reaching through the crowd to Jesus. I know that, in the end, he's good. He deserves all the honor and all the praise."

Yes, God surely molded Holley and prepared her for her present life, her new calling, her new world. Her time of preparation, her time of "molding" was a time when she could discover her gifts. Only the Potter knows the gifts yet to be revealed.

1. The National Alliance on Mental Illness (NAMI) reports that 25% to 40% of persons with mental illness will at some time pass through the criminal justice system. (nami.org)
2. Patchwork Quilt is part of the Northside Achievement Zone. NAZ is a collaboration of organizations and schools partnering with families in a geographic area of north Minneapolis to prepare children to graduate from high school ready for college. Students in the network are called "scholars" as an affirmation of their potential.

Caroline's Story

As she has moved into an ever-widening world, restored and renewed are realities Caroline has experienced in her own life and in the story of the hemorrhaging woman.

Caroline describes her life as a series of "do-overs." Transitions are a major theme in her story, from her birth in Kenya to moves to Canada and the United States, from motherhood at eighteen to her return to college and then to a promising career. Her spiritual journey, too, is a story of restoration and renewal on the way to wholeness.

Caroline was born in 1978 in Kenya to highly educated parents. When she was about eight months old, her family moved to Canada, where her mother pursued a PhD in education administration from the University of Alberta. After five years the family returned to Kenya, where they lived until they moved to Minnesota. There, her father, also an educator, earned a PhD at the University of Minnesota.

At the nearly all-white suburban school she attended from the sixth through the ninth grade, Caroline never fit in. There was little diversity and neither teachers nor students knew how to categorize her. She remembers feeling much more comfortable in the international graduate student housing where her family lived.

Caroline faced another major transition: her parents' separation at the end of her ninth grade year. She, with her mother and two brothers, moved to Minneapolis, where she attended Edison High School. The student body was diverse and much more inclusive. "I didn't have to fit into a category. I loved Edison. It was great," she says. Caroline starred in sports, especially in track. She was able to connect "with all kinds of people." She made friends across all groups and still values and maintains friendships she made at Edison.

In Caroline's family "college was never not an option." When she began planning for college, however, she discovered that she was placed into a category. She was classified as an international student, which meant high fees she could not afford. She was offered a track scholarship at a state university but could not afford to accept it. Private college turned out to be the best option.

Caroline attended Hamline University for one semester, but at age seventeen, she found that she was pregnant. She had to drop out of college. Her daughter, Cadence, was born in 1996 when Caroline was eighteen.

After working for a movie theater for a short time, she went to work for Campfire Girls and Boys, where she had worked summers as a student. There, she developed after-school programs. She says, "I loved youth development." Furthermore, she was making eighteen thousand dollars a year and thought she was rich!

Financial pressures, however, forced Carolyn to leave the agency after about two years. She went to work for the North Community Branch of the YMCA as the administrator for the president. As much as she loved her work on behalf of youth, she describes her positions as jobs, not careers. She also realized that she would not be able to support her daughter.

Caroline knew that a change in her life was possible when she discovered Texas College. In October she visited the college and in January she enrolled as a transfer student.

Caroline describes her experience at Texas College as "awesome." One of 119 Black colleges, its program was unique. Its mission was to enable single parents to complete their educations. Located in Tyler, Texas, with fewer than a thousand students, it provided on-campus support for the children of students. The children became part of the college community. Much of the funding came from the welfare-to-work program. The college was modeled on St. Paul's College in Virginia, which also serves single parents. Unfortunately, because of funding cuts, the college is no longer accepting new students.

Caroline remembers her years at Texas College as "the most wonderful time in my life." She describes the college as offering a "small family environment." Cadence also flourished, and Caroline says, "It was awesome to see the kids growing up." Caroline says that she herself was "super-involved." She was elected college queen and the president of the student government association. Even with her demanding extracurricular activities, she graduated with a 4.0 record!

As part of her business major, Caroline did an internship with the Target Corporation. On the last day of her internship, she was asked to continue her work on weekends and evenings during her senior year. This led to her present position as a project manager at the Target headquarters in Minneapolis.

Caroline credited two faculty members as being especially significant in her personal and professional development. President Dr. Billy Hawkins had himself been a single parent and had studied at St. Paul's College. "Texas College was his passion," she says. Of the campus minister, Reverend Clementine Gulley, she says, "She was my campus mom."

Caroline characterizes Dr. Hawkins as "very student-centered." She recalls how accessible he was during her term as student body president. She says that he was always available when she needed assistance. She tells how pleased she was when she saw him in the audience as she was speaking before the United Negro College Fund, running for the presidency of the Pre-Alumni Council. She knows that he had made an extraordinary effort to arrive on time for her speech. She believes that his support was instrumental in her election to the office. She summarizes her appreciation for her mentor by saying that working with him "formulated so much confidence in my ability to interact with top leadership."

Caroline describes Reverend Gulley as having "a harsh exterior" but being "loving at her core." "She took care of me even when I didn't know it. I couldn't have made it through Texas College without her."

Reverend Gulley was a liberation theologian. Coming from Kwanzaa, Caroline already had a background in liberation theology. When Caroline received a B rather than an A on her first paper, she met with the professor. She remembers having the feeling that Reverend Gulley was wondering, "Who are you? Where did you come from?" Reverend Gulley told Caroline that she had had students challenge a C or a D, but never a B! Impressed with Caroline's drive, she granted her request to rewrite the paper.

Caroline adds three more persons to the list of the top five whose influence has given direction to her life. Along with Dr. Hawkins and Reverend Gulley, she names Pastor Alika Galloway of Kwanzaa and her friend Loretta, a coworker at the YMCA who later joined Caroline at Texas College. Caroline says that Loretta's life paralleled her own in many ways. "We've been through a lot together." Last, but certainly not least, is her daughter, Cadence, who Caroline calls "the joy of my life." She says, "Cadence helped me grow up. She helped me get to where I am today."

Graduation from college meant more transitions. One was her return to Kwanzaa. Caroline had become a part of the Kwanzaa family before the church was chartered in 2002. Caroline had been invited to visit by her friend Loretta. Within a month she knew that Kwanzaa would be her spiritual home. She describes her parents' home as spiritual, but says, "We didn't go to church much." Caroline discovered that at Kwanzaa, "People genuinely cared about me. I fell in love with Kwanzaa and with Pastor Alika. I wanted the kind of relationship with God that Pastor Alika had." At the center of Kwanzaa's ministry, Caroline found "love and inclusion."

She remembers missing Kwanzaa during her college years but says that Pastor Alika kept in touch through frequent telephone calls. "When I returned," she says, "I needed to learn how to grow back into where I was before I left … and beyond."

Back at Kwanzaa, Caroline explored the differences between the spirituality at Kwanzaa and what she had experienced in the southern religious communities. She says that people at Kwanzaa are presented with a "blank book," not a book of rules. At Kwanzaa she did not feel regulated. "I was allowed to be vulnerable, to experience what spirituality meant for me." She describes both Pastor Alika and Pastor Ralph as "nurturing the spirit."

On her return to Kwanzaa Caroline was not allowed to sit on the sidelines. "Pastor Alika would not let me stay in the background." At the time of this interview, Caroline was fulfilling her ministry by serving on the session, chairing the committee on stewardship.

Caroline faces many questions as she looks into her future. There may be more transitions in her long series of do-overs: "I went from being seventeen to motherhood. I never had a chance to explore. I don't know what it is like to be a free adult. I skipped that whole stage, I always had to do what needed to be done. I don't know if I missed something."

Caroline reflects on her relationships. "I need to learn about building relationships, especially with men. I didn't learn vulnerability. That learning has to come later. That learning is a challenge."

Caroline's goals are intertwined with what she wants for her daughter. One of her priorities is building security for Cadence — emotional, physical, and academic. At the time of this interview, Cadence was twelve. Caroline has tried to teach values but knows that as Cadence moves into adolescence her values will be tested.

Caroline summarizes her concerns about the future by asking, "What do I want to be when I grow up?" She knows that she will encounter many new transitions. In addition to the challenges of parenting and a demanding professional life, she is working toward a master's degree in organizational management. She expects to change careers several times. More than anything, she would like to be married, to be a mother and a housewife. "I would like to learn what it means to parent with a supportive partner."

Caroline wonders about the time when Cadence will be an independent young woman. "I'll be forty when Cadence leaves home. What does Caroline's existence look like without Cadence? What will define happiness for Caroline? What will I do if I don't get married?"

There will be more do-overs for Caroline. Yet those who know her believe that, like the woman with the hemorrhage, there will be more times of restoration and renewal. "I want to trust God like Pastor Alika. I want to grow my spirit so that I can excite people about God like Pastor Alika can." These are the words of one whose life has been touched by grace.

Questions for Reflection and Discussion

- When have you found yourself in the story of the woman who touched Jesus?
- Describe a time when you were reaching for a wider world.
- How have faith, courage, imagination been part of your spiritual journey?
- How have restoration and renewal been part of your journey?
- How do you relate to this statement: "She could still imagine a life that was whole"?
- Who are the untouchables in your community?

For Further Exploration

- People who live with chronic illness or disabilities are sometimes told, "If you had enough faith, God would heal you." Yet, many who live with chronic health conditions or disabilities experience healing when there is no physical cure. What is the difference between curing and healing or wholeness?
- What part does inclusion in the church or community play in healing? See resources prepared by Presbyterians for Disability Concerns (PDC), a network of the Presbyterian Health Education Welfare Assoc. (phewacommunity.org/pdcdisabilityconcerns /pdcresources)
- What physical or mental challenges result in isolation from our communities?

CHAPTER 9

Living Advocacy: The Syrophoenician Mother and Peggy

The Syrophoenician Mother's Story, Mark 7:24–30

My daughter was dying. I was losing the child who means more to me than life itself.

A demon had seized my child and would not let her go. Sometimes when she lay on her pallet, her eyes dull like unlit lamps, I was sure that life had deserted her thin body. But when her eyes sought me to beg for water, I knew she was fighting the demon.

Day and night I cared for her. I was exhausted; I was desperate. I sought the help of the wisest healers, but she only got worse. I implored every god I knew, even the god of our ancient enemy, the Jews. I sacrificed to the gods; I made promises. I even tried to bargain with the demons. I promised my life in exchange for my daughter's. The demons only laughed.

My friends knew what I should do. They forced their advice on me: "She's only a girl. Give her up or she'll cost you everything. Then what will you do in your old age?"

When I refused, the whispering began. My neighbors became my judges: "Her daughter sinned. She offended the gods!" But what could she have done to deserve such pain? Some said she must have committed some terrible deed when she was in my womb. I could not believe that.

New rumors began to fly on every breeze that blew through our town — rumors about me! The townspeople gossiped that it was my offense that had caused my child's illness. Sometimes I even felt lecherous eyes following me, eyes that were windows into the wild imaginings of men who had always known me to be the faithful wife of my dead husband.

The hope I thought would never die began to struggle like a flame that flickers before it goes out. I was afraid — afraid that I would abandon hope. Then my daughter would surely die.

But the hope that everyone thought was foolishness burst into flame again when a traveler passed through our town telling stories of a healer called Jesus. The traveler said that everywhere Jesus went, people thronged to see him. We heard stories of lepers who were healed, demons cast out, people who were blind or deaf made to see or hear. But the storyteller's eyes grew wide and his voice became low with reverence when he said, "When Jesus speaks, it is like God visiting our people again. Many think he is a great prophet. Some of us think he is the Messiah!"

A few days later another traveler came through our village with the news that Jesus was in the region of Tyre, close to our town. My heart leapt. Did I dare to hope that the healer would come here?

My thoughts raced. I told myself, "Be sensible! You don't know whether this man was sent by his god or whether he is a trickster. And, even if he has amazing powers, he's a Jew! My people are Syrophoenician. We and the Jews hate each other. They call us unclean. They have nothing to do with us.

"But the biggest problem," I told myself, "is that I am a woman!" Respectable men don't speak to women in public. No decent woman — only a prostitute — approaches a man. I have no man to speak for me — no husband, no father, no son. Yet I knew I had to try if Jesus came to our village. My daughter was near death.

Loud pounding broke into my thoughts. Irritated, I rushed to the door. A small boy stood there, one who had often run errands for me. He was breathing hard from running. He spat out the words, "I know where the healer is. He is hiding, but if you follow me, I'll take you to him."

I looked at my daughter and watched her for a long moment. Her face was flushed with fever and her tiny chest was heaving hard and fast, as if she was wrestling with the demon who was trying to suck away the breath of life. The thought of leaving her, even to plead for help, tortured me.

But I had to go; there was no other hope. I wanted to run, but the boy walked, trying not to attract attention. He led me to the biggest house in the village, one whose owners could entertain an important guest. My guide motioned toward an open door and then disappeared. I was alone.

What was proper? I didn't stop to think. I stepped through the door. In the center of the room, surrounded by men, sat a stranger. I knew who he was.

I broke through the circle and threw myself at his feet. "I beg you, in the name of your God, help my daughter. She has a demon. She will die!"

Jesus drew back away from me. Maybe he was afraid I would touch him. Some of his followers moved closer, as if to threaten me. But the healer motioned to them as if he himself would send me away.

"Let the children be fed. It is not fair to take the children's food and throw it to the dogs."

Dogs! He called us dogs! I wanted to scream, "Don't you know we suffer too? If your God is merciful, why can't you show mercy?"

But then, like the burst of a bright light, I remembered the puppies, the puppies that scrounge through our village for food. They know where the best scraps are.

I had to take the chance. I had no other hope. If I offended him, what was lost? I plunged ahead. "But sir, even the puppies eat the crumbs that fall from the children's table."

I heard gasps of disbelief and shock. Had no other petitioner ever talked back to Jesus? I could feel the glowering on the faces of his disciples, the embarrassment of his host.

I dared one quick glance at Jesus. His dark eyes widened, his eyebrows rose as if seeing me for the first time. Astonishment? Anger? Irritation at being bested by a woman — and worse, a gentile woman? Or did the slight twitching at the corners of his mouth betray amusement, as if enjoying the scene of puppies scrambling under the table? My breath caught.

When he spoke, I heard no anger, no scolding. "For saying this, you may go. The demon has left your daughter."

Could I believe Jesus? I ran, not caring what my neighbors thought. I slipped on a sand-glazed rock and pain stabbed my ankle, but I could not stop.

Outside my door I paused. I listened for the wheezing of my child's breathing but, instead, I heard the tinkle of childish laughter.

I stepped inside. My child was sitting up on her pallet, giggling with delight at the weird contortions of the flying arms and legs of the clay doll she was bouncing on her lap — the doll she had been too weak to hold.

I gathered my child in my arms and she said, "I'm hungry, Mama," just as if she was waking from an afternoon nap.

I rushed outside to build up the fire for the oven. We would eat my finest bread, and we would give thanks.

Peggy's Story

The story of the Syrophoenician woman is the story of every mother who confronts power to save her children. If Peggy could step into the story of the gentile woman who confronted Jesus, the two mothers would have stories to share. Peggy's son, Cameron, and her daughter, Gabrelle, both live with learning disabilities. For many years, Peggy has been their advocate with God and with the schools. "Life would have taken a different turn if I hadn't entered into debate with God about my children," she says.

Peggy reflects that when the gentile mother challenged Jesus, he didn't chastise her. Instead, he entered into conversation with her, and Jesus himself was changed. Peggy describes her own role as "debating and believing."

Their mother's confidence in their ability has helped her children exceed the expectations of a society that often fails students of color and children with disabilities. Cameron's high school counselor told Peggy that her son would never graduate. Cameron proved this gloomy forecast wrong. After earning his high school diploma, he went on to graduate from Stillman College. Gabrelle's commitment to complete high school has led her to set new priorities. A basketball enthusiast, she gave up playing for extra study time. She is on her way to graduating!

Peggy understands her children's struggles because she herself lives with a learning disability. In elementary and high school, she was accused of being "lazy"; her brother and sister were the "smart" ones in the family. Neither her parents nor her teachers recognized her exceptional intelligence or her need for a different learning style. The schools made no accommodations for her.

One activity that was not limited by her disability was singing. She says she always loved to sing. She remembers, as a tiny child, singing "I'll Be a Sunbeam for Jesus" with the Sunshine Band at church.

Ignoring the advice of her parents and teachers, Peggy enrolled at Indiana State University. She did not do well. An astute professor, however, suspected a learning disability and talked with Peggy about it. This was Peggy's first insight into why she was struggling.

Peggy turned her anger on God. "Why did you make me this way?" she cried. Yet out of her pain she birthed a new relationship with God, one she describes as being very different from the popular religious notion that it is wrong to question or to get angry with God.

A new chapter opened up in Peggy's life when she and five-year-old Cameron moved from Indiana to Minneapolis. At Pillsbury House she found the opportunity to use her marvelous voice. The Sugar and Spice Theater starred her in two different roles. She played both Lena Horne, singing "Stormy Weather," and antiwar activist Angela Davis.

At Pillsbury House, Peggy's talents emerged in unexpected ways. A career in community service began when she was hired as a parenting specialist. Before she left Pillsbury House after eight years, she had been promoted to program manager and then to program director.

Much of Peggy's work has focused on women. She works with them wherever they are in their personal journeys. Her goal is to help each one understand her own vision for her life and then prepare to reach it. She says that women must know they can actually reach their goals. Her confidence in women comes out of her own experience. "I know what God can do," she says.

In her current position, Peggy is working with newly diagnosed AIDS patients. The Minnesota Department of Health assigns clients to her and her job is to connect them with the services they need. She describes her vocation as "an opportunity to empower women and men."

Peggy has years of experience working in both direct service to people with HIV/AIDS and in community education about AIDS. The neighborhood surrounding Kwanzaa has an extraordinarily high incidence of AIDS, but, Peggy says, "For the poor, any disease is a disaster." Her years as an advocate have given Peggy a keen understanding of the issues. She says that in working with people with AIDS, it is necessary to address other issues: mental illness, addiction, homelessness.

According to Peggy, building self-esteem is a major issue in AIDS prevention. Helping people feel good about themselves is a top goal for her. She says that young women, especially, use sex as gratification, as a substitute for the love that is missing in their lives.

As a singer, Peggy brings a unique gift to her vocation. She is the composer of "There's a Hole in Your Soul," a musical vignette she dreams of someday taking on a global tour. The hole, she explains, is a "God hole." People try to fill the emptiness in their lives with the wrong things. Only God, she insists, can fill the spiritual void.

Minnesota audiences hear Peggy sing in a variety of settings. She and Anthony, her husband of eighteen years, often appear in public with Danny, another member of the family. (Peggy says, "I come from a musical family and married into another.") On Sunday mornings they lead worshippers in songs of praise at Kwanzaa. When she has time, she acts and sings in community theaters, recently appearing as the Red Queen in *Alice in Wonderland* produced by the Urban Spectrum Theater in Minneapolis.

"We love one another," is Peggy's description of Kwanzaa. "Sharing that kind of love is one thing we do very well. We don't judge. We accept people where they are." She describes the pastors as teachers and says, "We use our minds." As an example of a challenging study, she recalls the *Red Tent*.[1] (Peggy is now an avid reader, having learned to accommodate for her disability.)

Prayer is central in Peggy's life. She recalls praying for and with her children every day before school. Placing her hands on their heads, she asked God to send the right people to them and to keep them from getting too discouraged. Her prayer for herself is that she will find a way to finish college.

Peggy describes prayer as "a personal conversation" that is not always "elegant." That conversation, however, has given Peggy hope. Like the Syrophoenician mother, Peggy has found courage to confront power as an advocate for her children.

---

1. *The Red Tent*, by Anita Diamant, is based on the story of Dinah (Genesis 34:1–31) and describes the lives of women during the age of the patriarchs.

Questions for Reflection and Discussion

- How did Peggy's experience with her own disability affect her relationship with her children?
- Peggy, like other parents of children with disabilities, has had to be a very strong advocate for them. How can we advocate with and for people with disabilities in our church, in our communities?
- Comment on this statement by Peggy: "Life would have taken a different turn if I hadn't entered into debate with God about my children."
- Do you believe that it is wrong to question God or to get angry with God?

For Further Exploration

- Given the status of women in Jesus' culture, how would you describe the Syrophoenician woman?
- What was the woman's ministry or gift to Jesus, to the church, to us?
- The story of Mark may reflect the early church's struggle as it moved to include gentiles. How would you describe your own church's ministry to people who are marginalized?
- How can the church be a healing community for persons who are living with chronic illness?

CHAPTER 10

Living Servanthood: The Shunned Woman and Geraldine

The Shunned Woman's Story, Luke 7:36–50

I was not invited to the party. I am never invited when the good people of our town, people like Simon and his friends, get together. Respectable people don't share their meals with people like me.

So today when I pushed through the crowd that had gathered to watch the party, I felt the stares and I heard the whispers, "Sinner." Some shrank back as if they feared I might touch them. Others pretended not to see me, as if I were invisible. But I'm used to that. If the religious people meet me on the road, they either look away or cross to the other side.

I didn't care about the guests or the crowd. I had come to see Jesus. Neither the whispers nor the stares could stop me. I wanted only to quiet the pounding in my chest and still the shaking of my hands. Would Jesus, too, shrink from my touch? Could I actually hope that he would accept the offering of a sinful woman?

Jesus, along with the other invited guests, was reclining at the table, his feet stretched out behind him. I knelt at his feet. I had planned to anoint his feet with the ointment, but what I saw stunned me. His feet were crusted with sweat and the grime of many hours of walking. Why hadn't Simon, that good man, ordered his servant to wash the rabbi's feet?

I cannot keep the requirements of our sacred law, but I know how important hospitality is for our people. I have heard that our ancient rabbis taught that welcoming a stranger is like welcoming the Lord. I cannot read, but I know the story of Abraham and Sarah. They entertained strangers who were really messengers of the Lord. So why had Simon, a righteous man, failed to honor and respect his guest?

As I knelt, my feelings of unworthiness and the sadness in my life spilled over into tears, great flowing tears I could not stop. Gently, I stroked Jesus' feet, letting my tears wash away the dust and trying to soothe the tender places. Suddenly the rising clamor of voices and the laughter made merry by good wine ceased. Not a whisper broke the silence. Everyone was watching me while my eyes were on Jesus. But did anyone offer a basin of cool water? When I dried Jesus' feet with the loose hair that marks me as a sinner, did anyone offer a towel? No, not one, not even Simon, who should have been thoroughly embarrassed at having a sinful woman offer what he had neglected. When I brought out the expensive ointment, the shock in the room was so real that I think I could have reached out and grabbed it. Everyone could guess the cost, and they were sure they knew how I had earned the money.

But they quickly lost interest in me. Jesus' enemies and those who were suspicious of the rabbi were watching to see whether my act would prove Jesus a fraud. I was only a tool. I was invisible again.

I knew what they were thinking. (I have been an outsider for so long that I have become very good at knowing people's thoughts. I have learned to be wary.) They were asking how Jesus could let himself be touched by a sinful woman. "If this man were a prophet, he would have known who and what kind of woman this is who is touching him — that she is a sinner."

Jesus, too, knew what they were thinking. As he often does, he told a story, a story about forgiveness and love. He said that those who are forgiven for many sins love much, while those whose sins are few love little. Jesus' listeners, of course, were thinking about my many sins, but I wondered whether Jesus could be saying something else. Was he challenging those who considered themselves the righteous ones? Was he saying that only God has the right to judge?

While the guests and onlookers were puzzling over Jesus' words, he turned to me and said, "Your faith has saved you; go in peace!"

Peace! My burden is lifted. I am forgiven. I am free. Jesus has shown me what God is like. How can I help but love God with my heart and soul and strength? God has welcomed me like a daughter who has been on a long journey but who has now come home. God has welcomed and accepted me. Will I find welcome in my town?

Geraldine's Story

Geraldine lives with the assurance that God has called her to a unique ministry, one for which her life experiences have prepared her. She knows what it means to be shunned, to be abused, to be rejected. "The story of the woman who washed Jesus' feet is my story," she says.

The daughter of a prostitute, Gerry grew up in foster homes and in an orphanage for girls. She describes herself as "thrown away ... given as a gift to an older man." She thought no one could ever love her. "Then," she says, "I graduated to jail." She was shooting up drugs and working the streets trading sex. She married her pimp.

"Don and I moved to Key West from New London, Connecticut. I was still working the streets at that time. Working in Key West was a great money-maker because of all the tourists that came through. I liked it because I didn't have to go out all week like I did back home.

"One night I went out to make my daily quota, and I put my favorite lucky red dress on. I usually made a lot of money when I wore it. I had a good night, and I went and got some cocaine. At that time I was mainlining. I was really high.

"One of the codes of the street is, never get into a van because of the potential things that would happen to you.... I met this man, and he had a white van and promised me there would not be any one in it but him. I got in. He played it off, like, 'Hey, you guys, I thought you were going to stay at the hotel.' I tried to get out, but they would not let me go. They said they would take care of me. They raped me until six o'clock in the morning and then threw me out of the van on the side of the road.

"I had no shoes on and my pretty red dress was bloody and torn. No one would help me. They laughed and called me many names: whore, slut. 'You deserve what you got and should be ashamed of yourself.' No one had a kind heart. I walked as fast as I could. My feet were hurting and I was tired. I needed to catch my breath.

"There were some church steps. I was relieved because I knew they could help me. As I sat on the steps and pulled myself together to go to the church doors, a clergy person came out. He said, 'Get off our stairs. We do not serve your kind here.' So who do they serve if not me?"

Gerry's life began to change after she and Don moved to Minneapolis. He was diagnosed with AIDS and given three to six months to live. He was in the hospital. Their financial situation was desperate.

At home Gerry went into the bathroom to pray. As she prayed, she rocked back and forth, kneeling in a puddle of tears. She was afraid that she didn't know the right words for praying, so she recited the Lord's Prayer. She discovered then that Jesus was right there with her, brushing away tears.

Gerry bargained with God. "If you save my husband's life, I will give you mine." She says that when she made that promise, she didn't know "my steps were ordered." She knew what she had to do. "God showed me the way," she says.

That was the beginning of Gerry's new life. She is now Minister Gerry. She says that she became a minister because she knew ministers who would not visit people who were living with AIDS. She says of her calling, "I don't go to shelters; I go to the streets."

She recalls that in Jesus' time, the task of washing feet was reserved for the lowliest servant in the household. Gerry says that this kind of servanthood has not been easy because foot washing is a task that requires no experience and gains no recognition. It requires only love. She did not recoil when a woman with boils on the soles of her feet came to her home. She washed and treated her feet.

Gerry's husband, Don, became a community leader, a strong voice for AIDS prevention, and an advocate for people living with HIV/AIDS. Together he and Gerry organized WUWA, Wake Up We're Affected, a community-based organization that educates about HIV/AIDS and offers support to individuals and families affected by the disease.

Gerry describes her husband as "a walking miracle." On March 22, 2008, he died of liver cancer, a result of hepatitis C. He had been coinfected with hepatitis C and AIDS, having lived with hepatitis for twelve years and AIDS for twenty. Gerry reported that his AIDS had been in remission for eight years. "We got the victory over that," she says.

Kwanzaa Church was packed for the funeral; many had to stand. The congregation included church members, community leaders, and many whose lives had been influenced by Don and Gerry's joint ministry. As a memorial to a remarkable man, sidewalk art in the Kwanzaa neighborhood celebrates and memorializes Don's contribution to the community.

Minister Geraldine now shares her own life story as she speaks on behalf of Kwanzaa's Northside Women's Space, a safe drop-in center for women who are trading sex, and as she serves as a spiritual mentor for women at the center. "If there had been a place like this when I was coming up, things could've been different." Geraldine's ministry continues — a witness to the power of resurrection and the promise of new life.

Questions for Reflection and Discussion

- If Geraldine had come to *your* church asking for help, what do you think would have happened?
- Who are the shunned people in your community?
- If we were faithful to Jesus' teachings and examples, how would our churches and communities change?
- Why is it so difficult to work for change?
- Does Geraldine's story make you feel helpless and overwhelmed, or does it give you more hope?

For Further Exploration

- In Luke 4:18–19, Jesus announced his mission. What do his words mean for us today? For girls and women who are trading sex?
- Prostitution and sex trafficking have been called slavery. What in Geraldine's story supports the use of this term?
- Dr. Lauren Martin of the University of Minnesota conducted the research that led to the founding of Kwanzaa's Northside Women's Space. She discovered that about half of the women first traded sex as juveniles, with an average age of thirteen. Many of the girls had experienced childhood trauma or abuse and homelessness. How can your church work with other congregations or community groups to put an end to basic causes of sex slavery?
- How are girls who are trading sex treated in the justice system in your community? Is treatment available or are they criminalized?
- What facilities are available in your community for treatment of girls and women in the sex trade?
- In addition to the passage from Luke, think of other scriptures that challenge the church to act on the problem of sex slavery. Some suggestions are Isaiah 58:6–12; Micah 6:6–8; Matthew 25:31–46.

CHAPTER 11

Living the Spiritual Life: Mary of Bethany and Rita

Mary of Bethany's Story, Luke 10:38–42; John 11:1–44, 12:1–8

My neighbors call me wasteful and extravagant. One of Jesus' followers accused me of not caring for the poor. But am I extravagant because I walked to Jerusalem to buy pure nard, the finest perfume? We are a poor people, but the nard was not for me. It was for Jesus. Am I wasteful because I used the perfume to anoint his feet? No! What I did was an act of reverence, an act of lavish love.

But extravagance is not the only fault that the townspeople find in me. To them, I am outrageous! When my sister Martha and I entertain guests, everyone in Bethany gathers around our courtyard to watch. They see Martha, the perfect hostess, rushing from one guest to another, refilling wine cups, replenishing the bowls of olives, and insisting that our that they dip their bread, again and again, into the bowl of lentil stew. When we entertained Jesus, she scolded me because I'm not more like her. Our neighbors gossip that I do not know my place.

But I know my place. It is at the feet of Jesus. I am a disciple, a learner. He invites me to listen to him and to learn from him, even though I am a woman.

My sister and I are not as different as you may think. We both know how important hospitality is to our people. Martha is always moving, but I know that she listens to Jesus as she works. She, too, is a disciple. She welcomes Jesus with elaborate meals; I welcome him by sitting at his feet.

How can I help but listen? When he describes the beauty of the lilies, I imagine myself walking in the hills around Bethany and seeing their delicate blossoms. I imagine myself breathing their fragrance for the first time. When he speaks of God's provision for ravens, I know that we, too, are in God's care. (Luke 12:22–31)

How can I help but listen when he speaks of the lives and hopes of our people? The poor in our land — and that includes almost everyone — yearn for good news, for relief form their hard lives. When Jesus says, "Blessed are you who are poor" and "Woe to you who are rich," we know that God cares about those who are losing their land to greedy men. When he says, "Blessed are you who are hungry now" and "Woe to you who are full now," we know that God hears the cries of those who are always a few crumbs away from starvation. We know that God cares about those who must beg to eat. (Luke 6:20–26) Do you blame me for listening?

No wonder our leaders are afraid and our Roman occupiers are always on guard. Jesus' fame has spread throughout our land, reaching even into Jerusalem. The common people throng to him for healing and for his message of hope. He understands our lives because he is one of us. He was a carpenter, one of the poorest of the poor. I wonder, did his family live in Nazareth because they, like so many of our people, had lost their land, the land that had been worked by their ancestors?

The future, especially next week, fills my heart with fear. After Jesus brought my brother Lazarus back to life, I saw the rage on the faces of some of the onlookers. (Why were they in Bethany? Had they been following Jesus, hoping to trap him?) They huddled together, angry voices shouting. I could not understand their words, but I didn't need to hear them. I saw their fists pounding the air, long bony fingers pointing to Jesus and then toward Jerusalem. Were they, too, afraid? Suddenly they were gone.

Jesus is on his way to Jerusalem. Our Passover, the time when we tell the story of our ancestors' freedom from slavery, begins in six days. Roman soldiers are always with us, but during Passover, our occupiers will be extra vigilant. Already, as we are preparing for Passover, our people are hearing the marching feet and the drumbeats, are seeing the Roman eagles high over their heads as extra troops move in from Caesarea. The power of Rome hangs over us like a boulder ready to crush our tiny nation at any hint of rebellion.

Our people long for freedom; they yearn to greet the Messiah who will set us free. Some of the rabbis teach that if all the covenant people keep our sacred law for just one day, the Messiah will come. Some of our young men long to fight, believing that when the Messiah comes, God will send a heavenly army to do battle for us.

Many of our people are whispering about Jesus, "Who is this man? Is he the one we are waiting for?" This is dangerous talk. Martha and I believe that Jesus is the Messiah, but one who has come to us with love, not with weapons of war.

Do you understand now why I gave such an expensive gift to Jesus? When I anointed his feet and dried them with my hair, my offering was a last gift of service and love to our teacher who came to us in service and love. Its sweet fragrance, the scent of musk, the scent of the earth, filled our home. All who love Jesus could share in the gift. Followers of Jesus knew in their hearts what their tongues had refused to say.

All conversation stopped. Even the townspeople who were watching joined in the silence. I breathed in a holy quiet.

Suddenly a male voice, loud and demanding, destroyed the silence. I recognized the voice of Judas Iscariot, one of the men at the table with Jesus. "Why was this perfume not sold for three hundred denarii and the money given to the poor?" (This was from a man who we suspect is a thief.)

Again, silence fell, not the stillness of reverence but of shock and confusion. The only voice I heard was a whisper from one of the townspeople, "Someone has finally put that woman in her place."

One by one, all heads turned toward Jesus — waiting, waiting, waiting. He was the rabbi who said he had come to announce good news to the poor, who had challenged the rich and powerful to do justice for the poor. Would Jesus reject my gift? Would he shame me?"

At last Jesus spoke, "Leave her alone. She bought it so that she could keep it for the day of my burial. You always have the poor with you, but do not always have me." He was on his way to Jerusalem. He knew why I had offered my gift.

But the scripture Jesus quoted about having the poor always with us doesn't end there. The Law of Moses continues, "Open your hand to the poor and needy neighbor in your land." (Deuteronomy 15:11) We don't have to choose between love for Jesus and care for the poor. Jesus taught us that we cannot separate love for God and love for our neighbor. This is the love Jesus taught and lived. How can I help but listen? How can I help but offer my best?

Rita's Story

"My love of spirituality" and "my love of learning" are Rita's immediate answers when I ask her to name her greatest joys. "They are my lifelines," she says. Like Mary, who chose listening to Jesus over conventional service, Rita's life experiences gave her the opportunity to choose spirituality as her highest priority.

"Spirituality is about hungering for God," she Rita says. Many varied communities, most of which were African-American Christian, have fueled her hunger as she "has struggled to know, trust, and love God as revealed by Jesus Christ." She explains, "Spirituality is about growing in the knowledge that God loves me and finally learning to love myself so that I can love others. Spirituality is all about love."

Rita named Jesus as her major teacher on her evolving spiritual journey. The Jesus she affirms as Christ, Lord, and Savior, she also knows as friend, brother, partner, mentor, example. For Rita, "He is the One who exemplifies what a God-centered, love-centered life looks like."

Her understanding of Jesus now is very different from that of her childhood. In sermons and Sunday school lessons she learned about "God's son who loved us and suffered on the cross for us." He was the One who knew our suffering — poverty, rejection, racism, classism — because he too had experienced dehumanization. "Jesus told us that God loves us and that nothing could separate us from that love. He invited us to trust God with our life now and in the future. I loved these messages from Jesus."

The pictures in the Sunday school literature and the imposing portrait of him near the pulpit gave another message about Jesus. This Jesus had "the whitest face and the bluest eyes I had ever seen." To a child, this was bewildering because the social context in which her community lived was very racist. White privilege was the rule of everything. Most of the families were sharecroppers, and the landowners were white and very oppressive. "They were certainly not loving," she says. "They wanted our labor but didn't want to pay."

According to Rita, "There was no getting around the internalization of Jesus as white. Yet we were trying to trust him as God's son and our lifeline to love and salvation. The message of the sermons far overpowered that of the pictures." As a child she was only vaguely conscience of this conflict. Many years passed with many life changes before she became fully aware of and was able to overcome the conflicting messages.

She traces her love of spirituality and learning back to her early childhood in rural Johnson County in Georgia. She had two younger brothers and two older sisters. Both sisters died during childhood, leaving Rita as the oldest living child.

Spirituality and learning came together as both were nurtured in her "home away from home," the Baptist church that also served as her community's school. She remembers the students doing the same chores for the church they did at home — dusting the furnishings, washing the windows, mowing the grass, and gathering wood for the stove. The teachers were all related to her family and she was popular with them because she was a very good student and learned to read early. This earned her an important place in a community where most people could not read.

Rita's childhood faith was "like breathing." Life revolved around the cycles of nature. People in the community talked to God as they brought water up the hill from the bubbling, cool spring below their houses, as they washed their clothes in the washtubs with scrub boards, as they encountered surprises or tragedies, as they disciplined children. "There never was a time when anything was separate from God." All of life was about spirituality and was basic to who Rita was even though, as a child, she could not have articulated this. Spirituality was "just life."

Rita's father was away from home much of the time, working on Georgia highway development projects. She was in elementary school when her parents divorced. She remembers this as the greatest challenge of her young life. In the years that followed, her pain about their divorce helped to shape decisions about her relationship to God and to the church.

For a single mother raising three children, church was more than church. It was the place that offered hope. Yet Rita describes her mother, who was recognized as a leader in the church, as "very spiritual but not religious." For her, what mattered was the way people lived, the way they showed their love for God.

Rita remembers the ways her mother experienced "the riches of spirituality." Listening to others and reflecting on their wisdom, her love for nature, a good visit with a friend, tending to her potted flowers — these were all expressions of her deep spirituality. She was able to ease a situation of conflict into one of peace in the community. She

117

loved to laugh at silly things she did. All this was as important to her understanding of the spiritual life as her participation in church. As we talk, I can feel Rita's excitement about her own relationship with God when she says, "For us God was everywhere and in everything."

Nevertheless, church attendance had a central place in family life. The pastor's prayers and sermons energized many family discussions. If the pastor offered a good prayer, her mother talked about it all week. If a sermon moved her, she was ecstatic.

Rita remembers that the songs of her people, the songs that came out of suffering, gave hope and strength. When workers tired in the fields, they would join in singing, "Go Down Moses ... tell ole pharaoh to let my people go." She says, "Oh, now that would just lift us up because we all had images in our heads of who pharaoh was and who the people were."

In high school Rita's teachers recognized her talents and her love of learning. "They became very interested in me and became mentors and supporters for me. They mentored me into and through Spellman College in Atlanta."

Coming from a rural area in Georgia, Atlanta was, in Rita's words, "something else." For the first time she confronted the reality of classism as she met students from privileged families. "I hadn't realized that there were African-Americans who lived like that. I was ashamed of my own background." In spite of the cultural shock, she fulfilled the expectations of her mentors and became the first in her immediate family to graduate from college. Referring to her teachers and family she says, "I am grateful to people who put a lot into me."

With required daily chapel, faith was part of everyday life at Spellman. African-American theologian Howard Thurman was a regular speaker at Sisters Chapel, and his messages challenged Rita to grow into a more intellectual expression of faith. In her sophomore religion class she had her first glimpse of Jesus as human and was strongly attracted to him. This Jesus of Nazareth,[1] a Jew, replaced the white, blue-eyed Jesus of her childhood. She says, "Oh, my goodness, I just felt that I knew him. He was, indeed, one of us." She was so attracted that she wanted to change her major from mathematics to religion. "You can't major in religion," she was told by her advisor. "You need a subject you can teach when you leave Spellman." So she continued majoring in math with minors in psychology and education.

Her teaching career began in Atlanta, where she spent four years teaching algebra and trigonometry to grades eight to ten. In early April she married her college sweetheart, who was attending medical school in Nashville. Rita learned to negotiate the airlines by making many trips to Nashville. By the end of her husband's senior year, it was clear to both of them that the marriage was on its "deathbed."

When the success of *Sputnik* alerted the United States to the importance of math and science, math teachers were offered scholarships to return to school for their master's degrees. Rita enrolled in a masters program in mathematics at Atlanta University. The sit-in movement in the country was growing. Rita and a small group of graduate students became active in civil rights activities.

Graduate school marked a new beginning for Rita, but at the same time, the ending of her marriage threw her personal life into turmoil. Her love of learning offered a sanctuary. "School was always a refuge when things were not going right in other parts of my life," she says.

Rita dropped out of church after her divorce. She was angry with God over her parents' divorce and over her own failed marriage. "It wasn't that I didn't believe in God, but if God wasn't powerful enough to keep my father and mother together and to save my own marriage, I didn't need him." Ten years passed before Rita "got hooked" on church again. In the meantime, her love for learning and her passion for justice led her along paths a girl from rural Georgia could never have imagined.

Rita married again, and after she completed her Master of Science, she moved with her husband to Norfolk, Virginia. She taught at Hampton University for two years. From Virginia she moved to Washington, D.C., where she taught in the public schools for three years. She was in Washington when the Southern Christian Leadership Conference and other civil rights groups organized the Poor People's Campaign and the March on Washington. The campaign planned for the people to live in tents, called Resurrection City, on the National Mall. She worked with the local committee to develop educational activities for the children.

As we speak about her work in the Civil Rights Movement, I ask about her hopes and expectations during that time. "I had all the romantic ideas that we were going to be able to end these injustices (racism and poverty). I thought if we worked hard enough, in a couple of years they would be gone. That's how naïve I was." I comment that this must have been a great disappointment. "I won't say it's been a great disappointment, but more of a great awakening," she replies.

I ask about sexism. "At the height of the Civil Rights

119

Movement, I hadn't even thought about sexism," she says. Later, when she confronted blatant sexism in another setting, she would have another "awakening."

"Classism is another big one," she says. "Every culture has its norms about what is worthy, valuable, and proper and what is not. I've had great challenges with classism too. I wasn't exactly a person who grew up in a middle class city family."

The Poor People's Campaign raised the conscience of some institutions about the issues of racial justice. Some increased their efforts to recruit more African Americans in their programs. Rita responded to an invitation by Harvard to apply for advanced studies in education. At the same time, her second marriage was ending. Again, her love of learning gave her strength, and she found refuge in her studies.

At Harvard she earned an Doctor of Education in curriculum development. After the Poor Peoples Campaign her interest had shifted more toward social justice, educational methods, and human development. "I became very interested in what was taught and how it was taught."

Rita and a group of other graduate students in education were given an opportunity to work with an inner-city Catholic elementary school in Roxbury. It was an ideal school for students who were interested in more community control of the curriculum and administration of schools serving urban African Americans. The school was on the verge of closing when the students arrived, full of dreams of developing an Afrocentric curriculum with parental involvement in the total program. Within the first year the school buzzed with new life. Rita called the school "the Kwanzaa of its day." Transformation was taking place in more ways than Rita could have imagined.

Teaching and learning at the new school were based on a philosophy that was revolutionary for its time. "We needed to listen to the parents. If parents had to listen to us about what was best for their children's curriculum, we needed to listen to them and see what they wanted for their children."

Listening to parents changed more than curriculum. It changed Rita in ways beyond anything she could have foreseen for her career — and for her personal life. The parents wanted the doctoral students to participate in church with them. Ten years had passed since Rita had dropped out. She says, "If I was to have any credibility, I had to comply. I was the director of the program."

So one Sunday she went to church, determined that this was the one Sunday she would attend. But going to church that morning was not what she had expected. "I went and got hooked by Jesus again. I remember crying and crying. I thought I was just having a weak moment. I went back and I went back. I had lots of weak moments."

Instead of attending one service, she began to go to the early morning service and again at eleven o'clock every Sunday. "I started to feel a transformation taking place in me — a full-blown transformation." She remembers being "immersed in a spiritual presence," "overflowing with love," and "wanting to change the world."

Her return to church birthed a new and passionate relationship with Jesus, the "Lord of Lords," the "King of Kings," the "Lily of the Valley" — the Jesus of all the accolades the church could offer. Her relationship with Jesus was evolving.

Years after Rita had chosen math over her love of religious studies, a call to ministry came through an unexpected source of wisdom. A woman who had been riding to church with her recognized what Rita herself did not know. "I believe you're being called to ministry," she told her.

Rita remembers the days that followed as "very frightening ... I wrestled and wrestled. I did not know what it was that had a hold on me." She questioned whether her call was mistaken. She was even afraid that in seminary she would lose her passion for Jesus and for justice. Finally she surrendered. "I just said yes."

At Harvard Divinity School, she continued her quest for the core of her relationship with Jesus. She earned her Master of Divinity, returned to her Baptist roots, and was ordained. She moved back to Atlanta as the assistant to the dean of the Spellman College Chapel. During that year, she was admitted to a doctoral program at Emory University. A major part of her studies was with Dr. James Fowler[2] on his program, Stages of Faith Development. The work at Emory helped her to integrate her studies at Harvard Education School and Harvard Divinity School into what she calls "spirituality and human development."

A call from the Presbyterian Church (PCUS) marked another turning point for Rita's life and ministry. The church offered her a staff position working with racial-ethnic education ministries. The primary focus was on supporting African-American, Hispanic, Asian, and Native American churches in recovering and living out their distinct cultural faith expressions as Presbyterians. She felt that she had at last found her real calling. "I was highly motivated and ecstatic," she says.

There were challenges, however. She was assigned to work in a team ministry with three male clergy persons: one Black, one white, and one Chinese. They decided to have a team retreat without her. When she found out about it, she was hurt — and then very, very angry." She asked the Black male, "Knowing what racism feels like, how could you do this to me?" He told her that he thought she would not want to go away with three males. He later said he understood her feelings and apologized. For Rita, that was a powerful, consciousness-raising experience for her on sexism.

After reunion in 1983, she moved to a new position in Black Congregational Enhancement in the Racial Ethnic Ministries Unit of PCUSA. There, she found the most rewarding work of her life. She had the great opportunity to work toward revitalizing African-American congregations. She describes her work as both "challenging" and "exhilarating."

A meeting at Johnson C. Smith Seminary in Atlanta brought together two strong women — Rita and Alika Galloway. At that first encounter, Alika announced to Rita, "You're going to be my mentor." In her staff position, Rita worked with Reverend Frank Vardeman Jr. to call Reverends Ralph and Alika Galloway to be pastors at Kwanzaa Presbyterian Church. Rita was truly a mentor, guide, and friend as the pastors nurtured an infant church into a vital community mission that one observer has called "a leaven in Presbytery." The support has been mutual. Speaking of Alika, Rita says, "She is an excellent pastor, motivator, prophetess, friend, and leader who keeps me going."

In 2007 Rita retired from her position at the PCUSA. "It felt like coming home to die." It was a time of "great sorrow" over leaving work that had given her great joy. She did not know what she "could be or do." Now, she can call her retirement "a time for discovering a part of myself I never knew." In her "new life" she has not lost her lifelong passion for faith, family, and justice. She is active in her congregation and in her family. She campaigns tirelessly for political candidates who share her vision of a world without oppression. She continues to be a source of wisdom for the many who trust her.

One of her convictions (perhaps growing out of her mother's rich legacy) is the importance of distinguishing between religion and spirituality. "Religion," she explains, "may or may not lead to spirituality which has to do with love, with how we express love, with how we live into love, with how we live into life through our relationship with God."

Rita remembers a single-page sermon preached by Dr. Howard Thurman at Spellman College as "transforming." His message was "Find the genuine in you." She recalls, "He spoke of God as presence in our lives. He brought out the mystic in me." She reflected that the older she gets, the more she realizes, "God is in all of us and love is that which is genuine in us." In contrast, she says that the church too often keeps us looking for God outside ourselves instead of within. "It teaches a lot about God's love for us, about loving God and others, and not enough about loving ourselves.

"I believe that if we continually grow in love with God and ourselves, we will automatically love others. Loving ourselves is continually choosing to give our bodies the best nutrition, exercise, and rest. It means overcoming our addictions. It includes sharing our gifts in community, loving God's creation, having good friends and family, and enjoying life in healthy ways. I am not talking about indulging ourselves with all the stuff of this culture."

Her deep and evolving spirituality has led her to move beyond the many clichés about Jesus and to ask again and again, "Who is this person?" She reflects on her relationship with Jesus, one she describes as "still evolving."

She speaks of the need to understand him in his own setting and recalls her own need to move beyond the white, blue-eyed Jesus of her childhood. She says, "We've taken him out of context as though his background didn't matter. Jesus was a Judean in northeast Africa. He may have been black or brown or paler. For me now, his color is not as important as his character and message."

Her passion for the triumphant Lord of Lords and King of Kings of the early days of her return to church, faded as she discovered that triumphalism was not the core value. She is grateful to scholars who "helped me see Jesus as human." For her, concepts about the humanity of Jesus are as important as those about his divinity. "What is most essential for me at this stage is seeing Jesus as human. His divinity may be the source of his humanity as it is for all of us. Full humanity may be more than we think it is. For me, to say 'We are only human' doesn't work anymore. To be human is both a high status and a high calling."

For Rita, knowing Jesus as a role model and an example gives us "an illustration of who we are and who we can be when our consciousness is focused on God as love. Triumphalism, by contrast, keeps us worshipping Jesus as God without seeing his humanity as our own. We can't hear Jesus saying, 'Everything I am, you are too.' " For Rita, Jesus is

123

friend, brother, mentor, partner, example. "Spirituality is about being a unique expression of God's love in each of our social contexts."

I ask Rita one last question: "What wisdom would you like to pass on to readers?" Her answer reflects her theology and her life: "To take ourselves very seriously, to love God and love ourselves as God loves us. If Jesus is divine and human, so are we, even though we will never know exactly what that means." She continues, "Stay hungry for God. God is love and justice. Being hungry for love and justice is the same as being hungry for God. We should understand love and justice as one word: love/justice. Our hunger for God will lead us to the next step."

1. The course was taught by Reverend Norman Rates.
2. Dr. James Fowler, whose groundbreaking research in faith development, is the author of *Stages of Faith: The Psychology of Human Development and the Quest for Meaning* and numerous other books.

Questions for Reflection and Discussion

- How has your faith evolved or changed during your lifetime?
- Who is Jesus to you? How has your relationship with Jesus changed since you were a child?
- How do you experience God as a presence in your life?
- How do you understand love and justice?
- How do you balance the need to be an active follower of Jesus and the need to grow in your own spiritual life.
- What does the word *spirituality* mean to you? Do you agree with Rita that one can be spiritual but not religious? Or religious but not spiritual?

For Further Exploration

- What do the following passages tell us about the humanity of
- Jesus? See Mark 1:35–36, 14:32–42; Luke 19:41–44; John 1:14, 11:33–35; 1 John 4:1–3.
- Why is the humanity of Jesus important in our understanding of incarnation?
- Why is Jesus' Jewish context and background important?
- Given the difference in the cultures of the first and twenty-first centuries, how can we know Jesus as guide? What are the basics in his teachings, life, death, and resurrection that can guide us as we make the choices that confront us?
- The writer interprets the story of Mary's anointing of Jesus to say that we do not need to choose between love for God and love for the poor. Mary belonged to a rich tradition that called God's people to "do justice, to love kindness, to walk humbly with your God." (Micah 6:6–8; Isaiah 1:10–17; Amos 5:21–24) Jesus' life and teachings were consistent with love for both God and neighbor. (Matthew 22:34–40; Luke 4:16–19) How is your congregation balancing the need for personal spiritual growth and the call to do justice?

CHAPTER 12

Living Hospitality: Martha and Virginia

Martha's Story, Luke 10:38–42; John 11:1–44

You probably remember me as the woman who cooked and served and fussed over her guests while her sister, Mary, did what was really important. I'd like to tell you my side of the story.

I invited Jesus to dinner, and I prepared a meal I was proud to serve: succulent lamb, bread I had baked from the finest flour, wine I had saved for special guests. I did it all gladly. Hospitality is so important to our people that we say that welcoming a stranger is greater than receiving God. So I welcomed not only Jesus but also those who always journey with him: Mary Magdalene, the other women, and a dozen men.

So do you blame me for getting annoyed with Mary for sitting while I was working so hard to make everything just right for Jesus? She was in her dreamy state, listening passively while Jesus talked. When I complained to Jesus, he said, "Martha, Martha, you are worried and distracted by many things; there is need of only one thing. Mary has chosen the better part, which will not be taken away from her."

Those who tell my story say that Jesus was scolding me for not being more like Mary. But I can't believe, for one moment, that Jesus was putting me down. Besides, who else did he think would feed him and his hungry crowd? After all, Jesus himself showed us how important it is to share food. He didn't let the crowds who followed him go hungry. If he cared enough to feed the multitudes, surely I could do my best for my guests.

To me, Jesus' words sounded more like an invitation than a reprimand. Perhaps he was inviting me to take the rest I needed. Or he may have been reminding me that my domestic duties don't need to be my only role. Many of his followers are women, and from what I can see, Jesus offers women the same opportunities to learn from him that he does the men. Unlike some of his followers, Jesus always treats women with respect. (I suspect that some of his followers use the story to keep women in their places, to make sure they are quiet, docile, and silent. I never have been quiet, docile, and silent.)

When my brother, Lazarus, was dying, Mary and I sent for Jesus. He didn't come until Lazarus had been in the tomb for four days. When Jesus finally arrived, we were performing the rituals of mourning.

I saw Jesus off in the distance, and, while Mary sat, I ran to meet him. I let him know how upset I was. "If you had been here, my brother would not have died!" Jesus answered that Lazarus would rise again. I told him that, of course, I knew he would rise at the great resurrection of the dead.

Then, as often happens when Jesus is speaking, our conversation took a different turn. Jesus said, "I am the resurrection and the life. Those who believe in me, even though they die, will live, and everyone who lives and believes in me will never die. Do you believe this?"

Suddenly the light of understanding flooded my being. What I had seen and heard from him filled my heart. Awestruck and trembling, I answered, "Yes, Lord, I believe that you are the Christ."

So you see, I had been listening too. Mary sits still ad listens, but I contemplate and pray as I work. As I open my home to my guests, I also open my heart. As I pour cool water over their tired feet and as I serve them bread and wine, I am seeing Jesus in their hungry and weary faces. I am learning wisdom from the heart of God.

Virginia's Story

Virginia learned to be a Martha as a child in a family that lived hospitality. The "whites only" barriers erected by hotels forced African-American travelers to find accommodations in private homes. Even Marian Anderson and Paul Robeson, whose magnificent voices thrilled white audiences, could not cross the color line. To them and to other distinguished African Americans, the Harrison Wilson family offered the grace of hospitality: safety, rest, food, and lively conversation around the family table.

In "welcoming the stranger" (Matthew 25:35) Virginia's family joined a long and sacred tradition: Pharaoh's daughter, who adopted the son of enslaved parents; Abraham and Sarah, who offered precious water to strangers in the merciless desert; Lydia, whose hospitality to Paul and Silas birthed a new church. Martha entertained the Lord.

When I ask Virginia to choose a biblical woman with whom she could identify, she does not hesitate, "Martha." She describes Martha as "strong, hard-working, and a woman who took care of her family." Then with a broad smile, she quips, "Besides, that's the name of my favorite sister."

But Virginia went on to quote the Martha who listened and trusted as she served. "Lord, if you had been here, my brother would not have died." (John 11:21) A strong and dedicated wife and mother and a woman with a lively faith — Virginia was a perfect "fit" for her spiritual foremother.

I first met Virginia after worship one Sunday at Kwanzaa. So many others were waiting to greet her that I stood in line for several minutes. True to her heart for hospitality, she actually apologized to me because I had to wait! After our conversation, the first of several interviews, we moved to the main door of the church where a friend was waiting to fold her wheelchair and help her into his car. He too had to wait as a group of young Black men crowded around to greet her. I was just beginning to feel the presence that has been Virginia's gift to the church and to the community.

She was the fifth child in what she calls a "typical large family" — four boys and four girls. They lived in Amsterdam, a small town in upstate New York. Her father, a brick mason, was often forced to work far from home, wherever he could find employers who would hire a Black man. But she remembers how much he loved playing with the children when he was home, as if he was making up for his time away. Virginia describes her mother as raising the children "almost alone." But she adds, "We all had jobs to do."

Hospitality was hard work. Virginia remembers the linens that were saved for the guests. After each visit, they were laundered, ironed, and carefully folded to be ready for the next arrivals. She describes the meals her mother prepared for guests as "nothing special. They just ate with the family." However, they often served what her mother called "cheap cake," a dessert that took only two eggs.

The children must have been all ears as guests and family talked around the dinner table. Virginia remembers that when their gregarious father was home, they "talked and talked and talked." She recalls that their guests loved her family. In return for hospitality, travelers brought news of a wider world where the Wilson children would later seek opportunities beyond what their hometown offered.

The family home stood among mansions along the Mohawk River. They acquired the home in a way that must have seemed providential. Virginia's father had done extensive renovation for a mortician who

128

inherited the house from a wealthy client. He had no personal use for it, so he offered it to Virginia's father for ten dollars a month! The enterprising family gained more than a new home. The four bedrooms and two baths made it possible for them to welcome guests. Every summer they welcomed Black college presidents who were on their way to the Catskills and Adirondacks to contact well-to-do donors.

Along with the daily challenges of parenting, caring for a large home, and entertaining guests, Virginia's mother encouraged the children to develop a sense of connectedness with the African Americans around the country. She subscribed to Black newspapers from Chicago and New York. "She wanted us to know what was going on." She was also knowledgeable about Black colleges and universities. She was preparing her children to live in a more inclusive nation.

Music and books enriched the Wilson's family life. An uncle who had a furniture moving business passed on books and musical instruments, the extras families left behind when they moved. "There were so many books," remembers Virginia. The family even gained a piano, which one daughter loved to play.

Despite the rich family life, Virginia describes her childhood as "a very difficult time." As in the rest of the nation, racism was alive in this small northern town. Virginia recalls that her brothers gained some recognition in high school because they participated in sports, but she adds that all the children faced "situations," the daily realities of prejudice.

The saddest blows to the family, however, came with the death of Virginia's three sisters. Two died when they were very young. The third died at nineteen when Virginia was in high school.

As soon as they were old enough, the Wilson young people sought jobs outside their home. Each eager, ambitious youth faced barriers to employment, but officials in the state government were active in encouraging companies to hire minority workers. Some of the Wilsons found jobs with General Electric in Schenectady, and the young men worked at the racetrack in Saratoga. But the Wilsons had bigger dreams for their futures.

Their mother had challenged and prepared them to reach for a wider world. Every one of the Wilson young people attended college, which shocked other African-American families for whom higher education seemed an unaffordable and impossible dream. Virginia graduated from Fisk University with a major in medical technology, a field in which she believed she could find work.

There were disappointments to overcome. One of her brothers earned a basketball scholarship that he had to give up to make room for a white student. He enlisted in the ROTC at the University of Indiana, served in the U.S. military, and went on to graduate from Georgetown University Law School.

Virginia met her first husband, Woodfin Lewis, after his discharge from military service. After earning his Master of Science and teaching physics at Hampton College, the couple moved to the University of Iowa, where he earned his PhD. During this time, Virginia kept busy raising two children, Ellen and Woodfin. When the Honeywell Corporation recruited her husband, they moved to Minneapolis where he worked as a research scientist until he died from injuries in a lab accident.

During the years that followed, Virginia called upon all the strength she recognized in Martha. A widow at twenty-nine and the mother of two children who were seven and eight years old, she supported her family by working at the University of Minnesota. She describes those years as "very, very difficult. When women ask me about being a single mother, I say, 'No way! Don't do it unless you are strong enough to fight the battle. You have to believe in Jesus and go to church.' "

She relates some of the challenges faced by a single parent of young adults. When Woodfin announced that he was going to work instead of attending college, she required him to pay his share of household expenses. Later, when with extra urging by Virginia's brother who was on the faculty at Fisk University, he returned to school. Virginia presented him with all the money he had paid, which she had saved for the time he would return to school. He is now, according to Virginia, a computer whiz who got into the ground floor of the high-tech industry.

National events presented other worries for a single mom. She describes the Black colleges as "on fire" during the Civil Rights Movement. Ellen, like her mother, attended one of the Historically Black Colleges and Universities. Virginia says, "When you are living in the Black experience, they take care of you." Nevertheless, when Ellen was at Howard University, "Bullets were flying." When Virginia cautioned Ellen, she replied like the daughter and granddaughter of strong women: "I'm not afraid." Ellen, who earned her doctorate in fine arts at the University of Minnesota, now teaches writing at Hunter College.

Virginia chose not to remarry until Ellen and Woodfin were out of college. Her responsibility for her children was her priority; "I knew I had to raise them." But when the time was right, she married Reverend Oscar Howard, a Baptist minister, community activist — and in Virginia's words, "a very loving man." Like Virginia's family, hospitality graced his life's work. Virginia remembers him as a tireless worker who was able to build his own business as an industrial caterer while he was serving the church and the community. She remembers times when, as a pastor, he rose in the middle of the night to be with a family in crisis.

After growing up in the cotton fields in Georgia, Oscar graduated from a culinary program at Tuskegee University. He moved to Minnesota and began the demanding work of building a business. Soon he was plunged into a central role in the Civil Rights Movement. When a leading activist asked him to serve meals to students at the sit-ins at the University of Minnesota, he agreed, although as Virginia remembers, "He wasn't sure what he was getting into." But his work for justice went beyond serving meals at the sit-ins. He joined with other Black leaders who were meeting with city officials to negotiate ways to get at the causes of the unrest sweeping through north Minneapolis.

The March on Poverty focused the attention of a nation on the inequities between the privileged and the poor. Oscar needed no headlines to pierce his conscience. The faith he and Virginia shared required him to act. A federal grant enabled him to plan, prepare, and serve three meals a day for an entire summer in several Minneapolis parks. Anyone who was hungry was invited, especially those who were "at home" in the parks.

Appeals such as "Can you send meals to my mother? She lives alone, and we know she isn't eating right ... " led to an extension of Oscar's ministry of food and hospitality. Virginia's eyes shines with pride as she speaks of her husband's vision of a service that would invite elders to enjoy nutritious meals — and more. To food he added friendship. He trained his drivers to go into each home, chat a bit, and make sure all was well. Meals were not to be dropped off on the doorstep! His program became Meals on Wheels, which continues today to enrich the lives of people who are ill, elderly, or recovering from surgery.[1]

Virginia speaks with something like maternal pride when she recalls the early days of Kwanzaa. She is too modest to say much about her own role, but together she and Oscar, like proud parents, were there from the beginning — he as preacher and she as the preacher's wife. As highly respected and honored members of the African-American community, their presence brought credibility to a new church struggling to be born.

Kwanzaa began with a dream for a new ministry, a Presbyterian presence in the African-American neighborhood in north Minneapolis. When members of the Highland Presbyterian Church realized that they could no longer serve the changing neighborhood, they did not move the church to the suburbs. Instead, they joined with leaders of the Presbytery of the Twin Cities Area in a dream of a new church whose worship and congregational style would be Afro-centric. They asked Reverend Howard, an ordained Baptist minister, to work with them in laying the foundation for the new church.

Virginia and Oscar began to gather each Sunday with a small but committed group to worship and to dream. Virginia calls Oscar "an excellent preacher" but remembers telling him some Sundays, "The only one you're preaching to is me." To this he would reply, "For where two or three are gathered together in my name, there am I in the midst of them." (Matthew 18:20 KJV) But the group multiplied, and with the support of the Presbytery of the Twin Cities Area, they called Reverends Ralph and Alika Galloway as co-pastors. Virginia is quick to emphasize and proud to say that she and Oscar "discovered" the Galloways. Years earlier, Oscar had assisted in Ralph's baptism. Later, he worked with him at Hospitality House, a community service agency. When Kwanzaa was chartered, it was the first African-American Presbyterian congregation in Minnesota. At Kwanzaa, church and community merge, as the life of the congregation has emerged out of its mission in the community. Hospitality, "welcoming strangers," is the mission at Kwanzaa. No one remains a stranger.

Getting together for a conversation in my home, Virginia refuses offers of help to move from her wheelchair to a chair at my dining room table. "I'm determined to be walking by fall." Her resolve came out of a lifetime of overcoming barriers: racism, single parenting, and later, poor health and impaired mobility. Her beloved Oscar died in 2006.

"I'm very grateful for my life," she says. She is proud of Ellen, Woodfin, and daughter-in-law Joyce. "I'm good because they are," she says.

"I am very blessed. I know what it is to be blessed." Yes, Virginia has been blessed, but she is a blessing to those whose lives she has touched. Hers is a hospitality of the heart, a welcoming presence. She has been a Martha, but her life also reminds us of another strong biblical woman. Scripture calls Deborah "Mother in Israel." Without exaggeration, we can call Virginia a "Mother of Kwanzaa."

1. For an excellent account of Reverend Howard's work in founding the program that became Meals on Wheels, see *Oscar Howard: Paving the Way for Meals on Wheels,* by Anna M. Rice. (section216.com/history)

Questions for Reflection and Discussion

- Are you a Martha or a Mary? Is it possible to be both a Martha and a Mary?
- What is true hospitality? Think about a person you know who lives hospitality. How would you describe this person?
- Describe "hospitality of the heart" that goes beyond offering food or shelter.

For Further Exploration

- Consider these stories about hospitality. What does each suggest about the meaning of hospitality? See Genesis 18:1–15; Luke 24:13–34; Acts 16:13–15; James 2:1–7.
- A midrash from the Jewish tradition tells us that God blessed the Egyptian princess who saved the infant Moses. God changed her name from Meroe to Bityah, "daughter of God." The story says that she sits at one of the gates of Paradise and blesses all who welcome strangers.[1] In Deuteronomy 5:12–15, the people of Israel are commanded to remember their own slavery in Egypt as they keep the sabbath. How welcoming is your church and your community to "strangers"?
- What would hospitality to strangers mean for your church and community?

1. Sasso, Sandy Eisenberg, *But God Remembered.* Woodstock, Vermont: Jewish Lights Publishing. p. 22.

CHAPTER 13

Living Tall: The Bent-Over Woman and Gloria

The Bent-Over Woman's Story, Luke 13:10–17

I am free! Thank God, I'm free at last.

For many years no one in my town has called me by my name. They call me "the bent-over woman." Now, at last, I will get my name back.

For eighteen years my back was so bent that I had to struggle to see anything above the ground beneath my feet. I looked as if I were carrying an invisible heavy burden on my back. When the village children saw me coming, they pointed, laughed, and raced one another to see who could run the fastest with a bent-over back. Some of the boys even made a game of butting heads like fighting goats. Then they would point at me and bleat, bleat, bleat until an elder finally stopped their fun and sent them back to their chores.

Sometimes at night when pain seized my back and would not let me sleep, I thought of the heavy burdens my people carry. Our backs are breaking under the heavy taxes laid on us by the Romans. Our people are losing the lands of their ancestors so the Romans can build more fine palaces. Our beautiful young girls must hide when the soldiers appear. How we long for freedom, and how I long to stand tall!

Then one day news swept through our village, catching like sparks on dry grass. Jesus, the healer, was close to our town. We had all heard the stories: lepers healed, the blind who could see, the deaf who could hear, the sick made well. Would we, too, see his wonderful works? Was he the one who would set us free?

On the sabbath the whole town gathered at the synagogue to hear Jesus teach. I couldn't wait. I pushed my way through the crowd, wishing I could stand straight and tall so I could see the rabbi. How I hoped that, even if he could not heal on the sabbath, he would bring a message of hope for our people. When I was close to the front of the crowd, I struggled to raise myself as high as I could. Pain stabbed my back, and it was all I could do to stifle a moan.

Suddenly I felt exposed, as if everyone was looking at me. I trembled with fear, wondering whether Jesus was watching me. If he was, did he feel my pain?

Then Jesus spoke, his voice calm and commanding, "Woman, you are set free." He stepped closer and I felt his hands, the power of his touch, on my back. My pain surrendered. My burden was lifted! For the first time in eighteen years, I was standing straight and tall! I began to shout, "Praise God!" I stretched as tall as I could so that everyone could see. The astonished crowd joined in praising God, and someone started to sing a psalm.

"Quiet! Listen to me! Stop!" At the front of the crowd, eyes blazing with rage, stood the leader of the synagogue. He tried again and again to quiet the crowd, but his shouts of "Quiet!" were lost in the celebration. At last the reluctant crowd quieted enough to hear him: "There are six days on which work ought to be done. Come on those days and be cured, not on the sabbath day."

But the crowd did not want to hear him. Surely our God must care about our people. Surely our God must know our pain. The crowd ignored his words. They were already carrying those who were sick forward to Jesus. The leader spread his arms as if to block the way. The uneasy silence that had settled over the crowd turned dark and ominous like a storm cloud ready to burst. Slowly, all eyes turned to Jesus ... waiting ... waiting.

In the distance a donkey brayed. Jesus pointed in the direction of the animal. "Does not each of you on the sabbath untie his ox or his donkey from the manger and lead it away to give it water? And ought not this woman, a daughter of Abraham whom Satan bound for eighteen long years, be set free from this bondage on the sabbath day?"

So that sabbath was, as our sacred story declares, a day of rejoicing, a day of freedom. I give thanks to God, and I pray for freedom for all our people.

Gloria's Story

From bent-over woman to standing tall — Gloria stands tall and lives tall. "It's been a long journey," she says, "but I'm happy."

A young sixty-five at the time of our last interview, she says, "I still have goals. I still have a bucket list." One of her dreams is to fly upward in a hot air balloon.

I can imagine the scene. As the gondola lifted and swayed and rose to meet the sky, a woman was standing, fit and trim. A halo of short-cropped hair, just beginning to gray, frame her fine features. Alert, searching eyes scan the horizon, but always sweep upward and beyond. Although bruised by life, she stands tall.

In recalling her childhood, Gloria says that her birth father left her mother because she needed to go on state assistance. Like most Black men in the 1950s, her father could not find work. By leaving his family they became eligible for the Aid to Families with Dependent Children program. When her mother remarried, it was to a Jamaican man who raised Gloria and her two siblings.

In high school she excelled in both academics and sports. Anticipating a career, she took courses in business and accounting. During her junior and senior years, she competed in girls' athletics. After graduation she enrolled in the University of Minnesota.

Her life took a different turn when she discovered that she was pregnant. The college social worker pressured her to give up her child for adoption. She asked repeatedly, "How will you take care of a baby?" But Gloria persisted. She was determined to keep and raise her child.

Still in college, she met her first husband. She says that she "settled" for the marriage because the man was good to her son. The relationship, however, turned abusive and after eight years she left him. After a two-year separation, the divorce was finalized. She was accepted into the navy, was accepted, but had to decline because she had no one to care for her son. Twenty years passed before she married again.

During her single years, she raised her two children, Russ and Monique, alone. She says, "I loved raising them as a single mom and would do it again." Nevertheless, it was not easy. She names the financial demands on a single mother as the hardest part.

Her long career in business spanned eighteen years at an insurance company and, at the time of our last interview, twenty years at the Federal Reserve Bank in Minneapolis. When I ask whether she had faced racism in her work, she recalls a problem on her first job.

A new supervisor took over the department where Gloria was working. One of her first actions was to take away the phones from her employees, in spite of the fact that they needed them for their work. She directed the employees to use the phone in her office and decreed that she would allow no personal calls.

This was unacceptable for parents who needed to be available for their children. Gloria received three calls: one from her children's school, one about a child's medical appointment, and one from a television repair shop. Gloria was called to the supervisor's office.

From behind her desk, her supervisor said, "You're not allowed to make personal calls." Gloria argued that the calls were necessary, not personal. When her supervisor would not listen, Gloria left the room without speaking. "I was afraid I would say something I shouldn't and get myself fired."

A manager, her supervisor's boss, summoned Gloria into her office and said, "I've never heard you get upset with anyone, but you left her sitting in the room. That's like telling her to shut up."

Gloria responded, "Yes, but I was protecting myself before I said something I didn't want to say." After her talk with the manager, everybody got their phones back. Gloria adds that her immediate supervisor "never liked me and would never promote me."

For Gloria, standing tall included continuing her education. While working at the insurance company, she was not only raising two children as a single mom, but she also earned a two year degree at North Hennepin College. During her career at the Federal Reserve, she enrolled in a degree program for working adults at Bethel University. At the time of our last interview, she was within a few credits of completing her degree in Organizational Leadership. Her goal is to open her own business.

Opening a shoe store has been a long-time dream. When I ask why she had chosen a shoe store, she answers, "I love shoes." She describes her store as a different kind of shop, one that will carry the hard to find sizes — smaller than five and larger than twelve. She knows that opening a new business will require solid research leading to a business plan, but she believes that her studies are preparing her for the next step. Her next step may be starting a new business venture with her son, who was a mortgage banker until the collapse of the housing market.

She married a second time, but, again, her hope for a happy marriage ended in divorce. On the eve of Mother's Day 2009, her husband accused her falsely of carrying on an affair. She ordered him out of their home. Loss struck again when her house went into foreclosure. Her husband, without her knowledge, had failed to keep up the mortgage payments.

Loss has been a constant companion for Gloria. The death of her sister, Cheryl, struck a devastating blow to the family. "Someday I would like to write a book about my sister, especially about the struggles my mother went through raising her." Gloria describes her as "slow" and says that her mother knew that after Cheryl's first baby, she needed to have her tubes tied. She predicted that her daughter would always be on state assistance. The doctor supported her mother's wish, but the state refused permission.

Within a single year, 2013, Gloria grieved a whole series of losses: a nephew, a close friend, and a cousin with whom she had grown up. An especially difficult loss was the death of her son's father, whom she called "the love of my life." In facing loss, Gloria has found support in close relationships with several other women. Some she has known since childhood growing up in Minneapolis. Others are members of her church family.

Gloria continues to face more challenges and changes in her life. Problems with her mother's health demand most of her time when she is not at work. Gloria has been present with her through repeated hospitalizations. Her mother's complex health issues have required her to use much personal time away from work, taking her to medical appointments.

Gloria calls her children, Russ and Monique, "the joy of my life." She speaks of them with exuberant pride. Russ has pursued a career in business, and Monique is a registered nurse and an attorney. After ten years of working as an RN, she graduated from law school and now works as a lawyer for nurses at a large hospital in Texas. Among her greatest blessings, Gloria also counts her five grandchildren: Taylor, Keyanno, Kennedy, Joshua, and Jackson.

Not to leave anyone out, Gloria says that she is really the mother of two-and-a-half children. Together, she and her mother raised Cheryl's granddaughter, Shanell, after the little girl lost both her mother and her grandmother. Shanell now shares in the care of the great-grandmother who raised her.

I ask Gloria how she has survived the bent-over times in her life. She answers, "How I got through the journey was with God. I prayed all the time. God's always been in my life. I've always prayed. I think praying, for me, is habitual. Two years before my last divorce I prayed, 'Show me the way. I don't know what to do.'"

Gloria grew up in a Roman Catholic family. As children, she and her two younger siblings went to catechism every Saturday. "One of the nuns told me that if I didn't learn the prayers, the three of us would not be able to make our first communion. She put pressure on me, and I memorized every prayer. The only way I could do that was to say every prayer every night, and, to this day, I still say those prayers."

Gloria remembers asking questions about the church at a very young age. She recalls wondering why she had to confess to a priest. She thought, "He's no better than me." Also, she questioned the celibacy requirement for priests and nuns. When her brother, the Reverend Ralph Galloway, invited her to visit Kwanzaa, she began a new spiritual journey.

One of Gloria's first services to Kwanzaa was greeting worshipers and ushering them into the sanctuary. Now she is using her culinary skills. Every Wednesday evening she prepares dinner for those who gather for prayers and Bible study.

I ask Gloria what advice she gives younger people. She answers, "I always try to tell young people, especially young women, 'Finish school before anything — any kind of schooling whether it's college or vocational. Travel a little bit, date, have some fun. Don't just settle. Keep God in your life. He'll steer you in the right direction.'"

As we review Gloria's life journey, I ask her to think about how she is different from the young woman who used to be Gloria. "When I was a young girl, I was shy. I was afraid of men. I don't think I am shy anymore. I don't mind speaking in public. I know what I want. I think I've always known what I want. I just have to apply myself to get there." And she has applied herself: single mother, full-time employee, mature student, family caregiver.

Through grace the bent-over woman was able to stand tall. Gloria, too, stands tall. When she climbs aboard the hot-air balloon, she will soar!!

Questions for Reflection and Discussion

- Who are the bent-over women in your community?
- What gives you strength to stand tall after (or perhaps even during) the bent-over times in your life?
- If you consider yourself an older woman, what advice would you give younger women? If you are a "young" woman, what wisdom would you wish to gain from an older woman?

For Further Exploration

- What realities in our communities, society, and culture are breaking the backs of women and men today?
- What is the meaning of "sabbath" today? What makes it difficult to observe sabbath time?
- Jesus was an observant Jew, but he put compassion for people above rigid following of the law. Can you give examples from his ministry? See Mark 3:1–5; Luke 6:1–5.
- Consider the prophetic tradition that valued justice, kindness, and humility before God over ritual. See Micah 6:1–8; Isaiah 1:11–17. What do you think these passages say to us as people of faith and as members of communities of faith?

CHAPTER 14

Living Transformation: The Woman at the Well and Tammie

The Woman's Story, John 4:3–30

I am the woman who the townspeople shunned. Every day when I went to the town well to draw water, I walked alone. I spoke to no one, and no one spoke to me.

But today I broke my silence. I had such good news to share that I ran through the streets shouting. I announced the coming of the Messiah, and they believed me. They listened to me, a woman they despised.

Let me tell you my story. Every day when the sun was high in the sky and the other women were resting, I went to the well. Alone, I didn't have to face their icy stares or overhear their whispering. They gossiped as if they knew me, but they didn't know my story or why I was silent. But I liked my time alone at the well. I could sit for a few quiet moments and ponder big questions like, "Does God hear the prayers of Samaritans like me?"

So today when I reached the well, I was so lost in my thoughts that I didn't see that I was not alone. A strange man was sitting on the ground beside the well. When I saw him, I was so startled that I jumped, nearly dropping my water jar. Anger surged within me. My solitude was spoiled!

My shoulders tensed. On guard, I stole a wary look around me. Were there others? I saw no one, but I felt the familiar stab of pain that warns me to be cautious. Only fools or fugitives travel the dangerous roads alone.

The man was sitting on the ground with his knees drawn up and his head bowed. Sweat was pouring from his forehead, and his sandals lay on the ground beside him. His feet were crusted with the dust of many hours of walking. I didn't know whether to draw my water or to run and raise an alarm.

Before I could do either, he looked up at me. Weariness flooded his eyes but I saw no threat. My shoulders relaxed a bit when I thought

I saw a hint of kindness in his eyes. He asked me for a drink of water, and I recognized his accent as Galilean.

His simple request stunned me. Good men don't speak to women in public. Besides, a Jew would never drink from a Samaritan woman's water jar. I wondered what the man really wanted. I could think of only one thing, and my body was not for sale.

Then he began to speak of many things, even about some of the questions that had filled my mind. He talked about God as Spirit who cannot be contained in the walls people build. We talked about my life. My panic returned. "He'll judge me like all the others," I thought. Tears of shame clouded my eyes as I reached for my water jar, ready to flee.

He did not judge me or call me a sinner or reject me as an outcast. Instead he offered me a gift. He called it "living water." At first I thought he was offering to draw my water for me. But when I looked around, I saw that he had nothing that would hold water. Well, I'm a curious person, so I played along, wondering what would happen. Was he some kind of trickster?

Suddenly, my heart burst open to receive his words. How I longed to drink from a spring that would never run dry! I opened my mouth wide and held out my tongue. I knew that the water he offered would be fresh and pure, not like the water that stagnates at the bottom of the well. How I thirsted for that water! How I longed to splash, to immense myself, to drink until I would never thirst again!

The truth washed over me, and I tasted the goodness of God. That goodness had been in my questions and my longings. The man with the living water knew my story and accepted me as one of God's beloved. I, a woman who was judged and shunned, now know that I am accepted by God.

Tears welled up from the depth of my joy. Awe, but not fear, overwhelmed me. How could I fear this man who had listened without judging? I bowed very low and my voice broke as I dared to say, "I know that the Messiah is coming and will show us all things."

He answered, "I am the one!"

I wanted to dance, to shout, to praise God. But before I could raise my voice, a group of men appeared, and I realized that they were the rabbi's disciples. When they saw him talking to me, they scowled, and I saw their eyes grow dark with disgust. Splotches of purple mottled the face of one of them. He looked as if he could barely hold his tongue. Nevertheless, not one of them said a word. Perhaps they were used to their master taking up with undesirables.

But their scorn didn't matter to me. No one could destroy the new life I knew. Besides, I had a story to tell. I ran into town. Even if the townspeople turned their backs on me, I wouldn't care.

I broke my silence. The words flew from my mouth. I spoke what was in my heart and they listened!

Tammie's Story

Tammie has lived inside the story of the woman at the well. "Jesus came and gave me living water. Now I don't just survive, I live," she says.

"The people in the town looked down on her. She was ashamed. She felt some of the same shame I felt. Jesus sent his disciples away and talked with the woman. She couldn't believe that he was willing to talk with her. That's the way I felt sometimes. I can't believe the Lord loves me like he does, as dirty as I felt. But Jesus helped her find the living water inside herself. She went away and spread the good news about Jesus."

The story Tammie tells about herself begins with shame, the guilt that she, a vulnerable nine-year-old child, took upon herself. Her mother was a hardworking single mom, so Tammie joined a big sister program. Her big sister invited her to go to Florida with her family. Tammie's mother gave her permission.

The events that followed marked and shaped Tammie's life. The woman's father challenged Tammie with "Can you keep a secret?" When she promised, he sexually abused her. Tammie blamed herself, sure that she had done something wrong. After all, her abuser was a minister, a "man of God." Tammie felt safe during the night only when she was sharing her bedroom with another person.

Tammie's fear turned to terror when her big sister and her father visited Tammie's home. They appealed to Tammie's mom to give up her daughter and let them adopt her. Shaking with fear, Tammie knew there would be no escape, no safety, if her mother agreed.

But there was no discussion. The request infuriated her mother. "I'm doing the best I can do," she raged, as she ordered them out of her house. The abuse ended but not the shame. Ten years passed before Tammie was able, at nineteen, to reveal the truth to her mother.

When Tammie was twelve, she moved with her mother, her brother Raymond, and sisters Melanie and Marina from Tennessee to Minneapolis. Her grandparents, her younger sister Angelique, and one uncle were already settled in Minnesota, where her uncle had been awarded a football scholarship at the university. Before Tammie's move, she missed her grandmother and begged her to let her spend the summer with her. Her mother gave her permission.

Tammie still speaks with pride when she recounts what she was able to do that summer. Her grandfather was disabled and was totally dependent upon her grandmother for his care. When her grandmother was hospitalized for a week, Tammie took full responsibility for caring for her grandfather and little sister, and for doing all the cooking and housework.

The summer was not all work. At the end of school vacation, Tammie begged her mother to move because "There is so much to do and the people are so nice." Her mother requested a transfer from her employer and the family became Minnesotans.

A new home did not take away Tammie's feeling of shame. As a teenager, she got into drugs. Looking back, she says that doing drugs gave her a sense of power. She believed that by using drugs, she could control her life.

She describes herself as a "binger," a preschool teacher who taught five days a week and got high on weekends. She estimated that in twenty years she missed only five to ten days of work. I ask her how she got free of drugs. "I got tired," she says. She had already gone through treatment three times and, each time, she relapsed.

Finally, the breakthrough came. She discovered the Lydia Project[1] and Kwanzaa Church. At Lydia she found sisterhood, women who had faced challenges that threatened to overcome them. At Kwanzaa she found support in the love she had been seeking. Together they gave her the strength to get off and stay off drugs.

She had visited several other churches seeking forgiveness but, when she shared her story, she met only judgment. "If they weren't forgiving, I didn't need to be there. I was already struggling with forgiving myself. So for a few years I was lost."

Finally, she tried Kwanzaa, visiting for the first time with her brother and sister-in-law. ("They needed a force to go with them!" she says.) She may have attended reluctantly, but she says, "I don't know what it was, but as soon as I walked in the door, God told me I was home."

145

Even in her new home, at first it wasn't easy for Tammie. She was still fearful about talking with people. For a while she and her mother attended worship together, but Tammie fled to her car right after the last song. She would tell her mom, "I'll wait for you in the car." Finally her wise mother said, "You need to start talking to people."

"My life began to change," Tammie says. "While I was working on trying to forgive myself, I was seeing all those people who were comfortable at church, all those people God had forgiven. The more I came, the more I started to forgive myself. I wasn't a person to go up front,[2] but I remember going forward and asking for prayer one Sunday."

At Kwanzaa Tammie discovered that people were free to tell their stories. There was no judgment. She found a friend in a woman who was working as a substance abuse counselor at the African-American Family Center. Her new friend had gone through many of the same struggles. She too was a "woman at the well."

Telling her story began to lift Tammie's burden. "Who am I not to love me when a man [Jesus] so great does?" She found the freedom to share her story with others, as she did during our conversation.

She surrendered her life to Christ. "I knew then that everything I did was going to be about him. I became a better mother, a better daughter, a better person."

Tammie's faith has not protected her from pain — or even anger with God. She cried, "Why my family?" when her niece and her sister, Angelique, were diagnosed with breast cancer. Again, sharing with a friend helped. Her prayer about her sister's illness changed. "Lord, be with us. If it's your will to bring her home, be with us. Let the family know that you are their comforter. Guide us about what we are supposed to do with her children."

Tammie finds great joy in her daughters, Miesha and TaSheria, and in her six grandchildren. One grandchild lives with cerebral palsy, but Tammie has discovered the unique gifts he has brought to the family and the church. When the congregation is praising God in worship through music, he dances down the aisle. When he embarrasses his big sister, Tammie tells her, "He can praise God however he wants. Look at God working."

Like her spiritual foremother, the woman at the well, Tammie is telling the good news about Jesus in words and in action, in church and in the community. She is a ruling elder at Kwanzaa and represents the church at neighborhood action groups. She even discovered recently that she could plan and prepare meals for 140 students and staff at a community Freedom School.[3] With her love for children, she was also the ideal teacher for a class of "junior chefs" who learned to make pizza, rice cereal bars, and other kids' favorites.

But another life transition has been a source of healing for Tammie. During our last conversation she describes her work at PRIDE[4] as an advocate for women who have been sexually assaulted. "We work to help women who have been exploited and traded and trafficked to move forward to a better life. In trauma healing groups we help women to get past and to heal from the trauma of sex exploitation." In helping other women heal, Tammie has discovered new inner strength for herself. "I love my work. It is my passion. In my work I have found healing from what I have lived through.

"I'm put on this earth to help people," she says. "This is who I am. We are blessed so we can bless someone else." She has become the person she is today out of her own pain and the peace she has found at the well, the living water offered by Christ.

1. The Lydia Women's Empowerment Project was organized by Reverend Paula Sanders with a Self Development of People grant. The women learned sewing and textile arts and created stole and liturgical hangings. As they sewed, their spiritual lives were enriched through Bible study, sharing of personal stories, and prayers.
2. As a response to the ministry of music, the reading of scriptures, and preaching, worshippers are invited to come forward to ask for prayers or to unite with the church.
3. Freedom Schools are African-American summer literacy programs and are held in cooperation with the Children's Defense Fund. The first Freedom Schools were organized in the South by civil rights workers.
4. From PRostitution to Independence, Dignity, & Equality. PRIDE provides support services to individuals and families that include counseling, support groups, legal advocacy, referrals, case management, education, and system advocacy.

Questions for Reflection and Discussion

- When you think of water, what words, scenes, sounds, or memories come to mind? Do any of these describe "living water"?
- Why do you think so many biblical writers used water as a symbol for life or new life? (Remember that water was scarce and precious in the biblical setting.)
- What did "living water" mean to the Samaritan woman? To Tammie?
- What does "living water" mean to you?
- When, where, or how do we receive the gift of "living water?"

For Further Exploration

- What do each of the following passages from scripture say about the water that gives and renews life? (Isaiah 12:3; Jeremiah 17:7–8; John 4:13–14, 6:35, 7:37–39; Revelation 22:17)
- After her encounter with Jesus, the woman who had been shunned returned to her village with good news. Many of the stories of Jesus' acts are about restoration of persons to the community. The New Testament culture was communal rather than individualistic. What does 2 Corinthians 5:17–18 say to those who have received the gift of new life? See also The Confession of 1967, 9:06–07.
- As a child, Tammie was afraid to tell her mother about her abuser. What can churches do to provide safe settings for children and adults who are being abused?

CHAPTER 15

Living Leadership: Lydia, the Slave Girl, and Beverly

Lydia's Story, Acts 16:11–15

My women and I are marked. Our hands, our wrists, our arms — we can never scrub them clean of the purple that marks us.

We dye and sell purple cloth, but we never wear purple. Wearing purple marks the rich and the noble. We are people who work with our hands, those the Romans call *sordidum*. We are the underclass. We work from dawn until dark until we think our backs will break. But people who work with their hands never rise to a higher rank.

Our city, Philippi, is a colony for veterans of Caesar's wars. The Pax Romana prevails — the Roman Empire's way of peace. In this system my rank will never change. I will always be marked as a woman of the lower classes.

Yesterday a buyer for an aristocrat came to examine our cloth. I knew that he recognized the richness, the beauty, the fine workmanship, but he only sniffed and wrinkled his nose as if he were afraid he might be assaulted by some foul odor. He pretended that our cloth didn't meet his superior standards. But I knew what lay behind his airs: he was trying to cheat us out of a fair price.

I know how luxurious our cloth is, even though many consider the dye made from the madder root less brilliant than the color from the sea snail. I know better. My women and I are marked, but we are skilled. As we work together, I love to see the color emerging as we soak the cloth in the running water of the Gangites River. I touch, I stroke, I caress the brightly colored wool, rolling it gently and tenderly through my fingertips. Sometimes when no one is watching, I drape my body, imagining that I am a great lady. But, the purple I wear will always be the purple that marks me, the purple I wear on my skin.

But I am marked in another way, a way that is invisible. I am a worshipper of the God of Jesus, not the gods of the empire. Before I became a believer in Jesus, I was one the Jews call a seeker. I learned about the God of Jesus from a Jew named Judith.

I used to ask her why she didn't burn incense or sacrifice to the Roman gods. I asked why she can't have many gods like the Romans do. She told me that there is only one God, the Lord of the Universe.

So she began to tell me stories of her people. She told me about Moses and Miriam leading their people out of slavery into freedom. She told me about the prophets who demanded righteousness and justice in the name of their god. What she told me about her god was different from the Roman gods who have to be teased and bribed by mortals. I searched my heart and I knew that I had to worship the Holy One, the one God.

So my women and I began to pray on the seventh day, the Jewish sabbath. We pray at the riverside where we work. It seems only natural because as we work, we tell our stories, we sing, we laugh, we celebrate. Sometimes we weep for one another. Our place of prayer is not a usual kind of synagogue — that requires ten men. We are women, marked women, praying outside the city gates.

I have assured myself and my women that we are in a safe place, away from the leering eyes of Roman men or the suspicious fantasies of those who have power over us. Yet I am always wary, forever alert. Sometimes I feel as though an unseen presence, like a stealthy beast, is crouching outside our circle, prepared to strike at some unguarded moment.

So you will not be surprised when I tell you that my stomach clenched and my shoulders stiffened when my fears took on the shape of two strangers. They appeared suddenly while we were praying on the last sabbath. I tried to take in everything about them as I motioned my women, trying to assure them that all would be well. The men's faces were bronzed and furrowed as if beaten by many days of wind and sun. They wore the rough clothing of workers, and their sandals were worn. I knew they were not buyers for a rich client. Their hands bore the calluses of hard labor. Our God requires hospitality, so I stepped forward and bowed, trying to quiet the pounding in my chest and still the shaking of my voice. I offered something to eat and drink and a place to rest.

One of the men spoke. He introduced himself as Paul and his companion as Silas. His voice was not that of either a ruffian or an aristocrat. I was puzzled because he seemed a learned man who worked with his hands. He answered that it was not food, drink, or a place to rest they wanted. Instead, they wished only to pray with us. They wanted to pray with women!

My mind raced. Who were these two? Why didn't they join the men in their synagogue if they really wanted to pray? Were they fugitives, running from the Roman law? Were they, too, marked? Still wary, I welcomed the men and we prayed together, a group of women and two strange men.

Then Paul took the place of a teacher. He sat as teachers do in a synagogue. He taught us about a man called Jesus. He told us that the God we worship sent Jesus into the world but that the Romans crucified him as they do traitors. But Paul announced the good news. God raised Jesus from death!

He said that in Jesus, God broke down the walls that divide us. Paul said that God invites all of us to believe in Jesus and to be baptized. We become one in Christ.

Paul's words were convincing, but it was my own heart that spoke to me. I felt a new Spirit calling to my spirit. My heart told me that the God I worship had chosen Jesus to bring light and new life into the world. I had to trust my heart. I had to trust the Spirit within me.

What a celebration it was! My household, my women, and I were baptized into that beloved community that I know reaches far beyond my own household. Paul called the community of believers — rich or poor, slave or free, male or female, Jew or Gentile — the Body of Christ.

Paul said we all have gifts to use in the service of Christ. One of my gifts is hospitality. I insisted (I would not let them say no) that Paul and Silas stay in my home as long as they are working in Philippi. The new church will meet in my home.

But my women and I share another gift. We use our marked hands and arms to create beauty to glorify the God of Jesus, the One whose hands and sides were marked by suffering. God was in Jesus and we know that Christ dwells in us. Thanks be to the God of Jesus!

The Slave Girl's Story, Acts 16:16–19

I was a slave — nothing more. My chains were invisible, but my masters' fierce greed held my spirit captive. But I am no longer useful to them; they have abandoned me. I am free, but ...

Everything changed for me when two men — they're called Paul and Silas — came to Philippi. They preached about Jesus. They said their God sent Jesus to save the world, but the Romans crucified him. That was not the end of the story. The good news is that God raised him from the dead! Their god must be very powerful — more powerful than our Roman gods. Our Caesars call themselves "Lord" and "Savior," but they can't rise from the dead! Something deep inside me told me that Paul and Silas were telling the truth.

That is how I got into trouble with my masters. I was a fortune-teller, and I made them rich. People paid big money to hear the words that came from my mouth. When we paraded through the streets, my masters went ahead shouting, "Discover your future! Hear what our great god Apollo has to tell you!"

I know that my masters' eyes were always shifting, as if hunting for prey. Even a poor man jiggling a few coins was a target for the hunt. But if my owners sighted a man wearing an especially fine toga or someone guarded by many slaves, they moved in for their prey, eager to relieve him of his wealth. They always promised riches, beautiful women or boys, and more manhood if they could discover their future. (This promise was always meant to be fulfilled after negotiating a suitable sum.)

So they came to me — the poor and the rich, the common and the powerful, the gullible and even the cynics. They asked if they should buy property, take wives, or go to war. I saw the expectation in their eyes. In my heart I pitied the poor who came, hoping for a better life.

When I fell into a trance, they believed the god Apollo was speaking through me. They pondered, debated, and examined every word because the words from my mouth were always mysterious, like riddles. That way no one could say the message was false or accuse my masters of a fraud. My owners could always claim that their accuser had not understood the god's message.

So my masters got rich. They lived in the finest villas in the city. I slept — when I wasn't too cold, too afraid, or too hungry — in a shack with other slaves. Sometimes I raced the dogs for scraps of food my masters tossed from their tables when their bellies were bulging.

No wonder my masters hate Paul and Silas! My heart told me that their message was from the great God. I found my own voice when I heard their good news.

152

So when my masters shouted to sell my services, I shouted even louder. I, too, could announce the good news: "Paul and Silas are the slaves of the Most High God, who proclaims to you a way to salvation."

Instead of being pleased, however, Paul was annoyed! Why? I thought if Jesus had been there, he would have been pleased, not irritated. He must be a good man sent by a God who cares about people like me. The Roman gods care nothing about slaves or people who beg for food or sleep in the streets.

But Paul, irritated as he was, said to my fortune-telling spirit, "I order you in the name of Jesus Christ, to come out of her." His words broke the chains that held me. I flung my arms wide to welcome my new Spirit. I knew I would tell no more fortunes.

My masters fumed with anger. They grabbed me and dragged me away by my hair. My ears are still ringing with the curses they screamed. Finally, hurling a last curse, they flung me to the ground. They knew I was of no more use to them.

They seized Paul and Silas, and dragged them to the authorities. (Maybe Paul had been afraid of trouble, and that's why he wanted me to be quiet.) I suspect that Paul and Silas are in prison now. My masters are powerful men.

I have a new Spirit inside me. But where will I go? Will I have to beg? Will I have to sell my body to eat?

I have one hope. I've heard about a gathering of women by the riverside outside the city. They work for a woman named Lydia making purple cloth, but I've heard that they also pray together. I've heard rumors that they know about Jesus too. I've even heard that Paul and Silas have been staying at Lydia's house.

Maybe I can learn to make purple cloth and work with them. Maybe I can pray with them. Then I'll be truly healed!

Beverly's Story

Beverly is a twenty-first-century Lydia: entrepreneur, church officer, worship leader. Her life is marked by gratitude.

We don't know whether Lydia could sing, but when Beverly lifts her magnificent voice in praise at Kwanzaa, the sound swells to fill the sanctuary. When she tells her story, she seasons it with both humor and a sense of blessedness. "I'm so grateful, so very grateful," she says.

Beverly says that "a whole lot of things" shaped her life and made her the person she is today. She grew up in a south Minneapolis neighborhood of both homes and shops. Her family lived across the street from a potato chip factory. That meant free potato chips for children who were scavenging for treats!

The appearance of a large trunk in the foyer of the family home marked a change for the family. Beverly says that what was happening was "above a child's understanding." At first she thought nothing about the trunk but soon she overheard her mother saying that her father was moving out.

Beverly remembers her exuberant father being unusually quiet and calm. She realized later that he was doing his best to control his emotions. She remembers her prim mother standing straighter and taller than usual.

Beverly's father did not disappear from her life. "My dad was always close … always around me." He always lived nearby, renting a room above a neighborhood barbershop. When Beverly and her mother moved across the city to north Minneapolis, he followed and rented a room in the home of her mother's pastor. Beverly describes her parents as good friends in spite of their differences.

Beverly calls her mother a "church lady." She always attended the church conventions, and for years she always wore white to services. After they joined a Pentecostal church, her mother discovered that they could go to church wearing colors.

She describes her father as "wild." "He loved to dance and go to clubs and he loved younger women." Beverly remembers telling him that even though he liked young women, he shouldn't be giving them all his money.

Some of the women whose company her father enjoyed lived upstairs above a corner pharmacy. The children ran, played, and climbed on woodpiles behind the building. "The women really liked us," Beverly says. "They would hang out the windows and call, 'Honey, you want this?' Then, they would throw their old costume jewelry out the window."

The children took their bounty to their clubhouse where they "pranced and paraded" with their treasures. The fun continued until Beverly's mom discovered their jewelry and realized where it had come from. She "hit the ceiling." Beverly says that, eventually, she too was able to "put two and two together."

154

During her childhood, music surrounded Beverly and filled her life. Her mother and grandmother were both singers, and Beverly's love of singing was nurtured by spending long hours listening to Mahalia Jackson on old seventy-eight phonograph records. Mahalia's rich tones shaped the young singer's voice and style. Beverly says she learned to sing from Mahalia and church choirs. When she was seven, she joined her first choir, at Soul's Harbor in downtown Minneapolis.

Beverly's mother insisted that she learn a trade, dressmaking. So when she was nineteen, she began three years of training at a vocational school in Minneapolis. She learned not only dressmaking but also design, tailoring, and millinery. Beverly, however, had broader interests and her world began to expand.

Working as a receptionist at the Minneapolis Urban League, she met the Reverend Maxie Turner. He called her "child" and "daughter." For Beverly, Maxie was her "second dad" and her "spiritual father." Beverly considers herself "blessed to have had two dads" and says that her "real" dad was "cool" with her relationship with Reverend Maxie.

Beverly credits Reverend Maxie with teaching her table manners. She says that her "very prim and proper" grandmother taught her etiquette but Reverend Maxie "made it current." She remembers having tea with him and hearing him say things like, "This is the way to squeeze the tea bag."

When Beverly and her boyfriend decided to get married (after three failed attempts), Reverend Maxie learned of their intent to appear before a justice of the peace. He was "appalled" and considered this a personal insult because he was licensed to officiate at weddings. So Reverend Maxie not only married the couple, he even hosted the wedding in his home. Beverly walked down the stairs in a white dashiki she had designed and sewn. Both her garments and the white dashiki worn by the groom were decorated with red, proclaiming, "Power to the people!"

The marriage lasted for twenty-three years — ten years too long, according to Beverly. She says the marriage "deteriorated," especially after her husband's diagnosis of diabetes. He had been a track star, a "big man on campus," but after his diagnosis, "He began to do everything he shouldn't do." He left the family three times before the breakup became final. A long recovery followed for Beverly and the children.

"I've been in so many situations. It could have been *Miami Vice*," she says. In 1970 Beverly, her mother, brother, and a seven-day-old infant barely escaped being blown up. They were home during a violent storm. They heard a blast. They thought it was lightning. Then they saw the front of their home — blown to bits! Later the police discovered the cause of the blast. A young man walking past Beverly's house was carrying a bomb. It detonated in the storm!

Beverly could have starred in another television series. For seven months she was held in a Caribbean prison. If the walls of her cell had been able to speak, they could have told stories of the African slaves who were imprisoned and tortured. They could not speak, but the holes that anchored chains to the walls gave silent witness to the suffering of the prisoners. Two streams of history merged in that cell: the age of slavery and the ongoing struggle for human rights. After her release Beverly testified before a United Nations Committee investigating human rights.

Life back in Minnesota was not as dramatic, but it was still challenging. A community activist, she ran for Minneapolis City Council from the Eighth Ward and was elected twice to the Neighborhood Revitalization Policy Board, which was part of a twenty-year plan. As a corporate financial officer first for a bank and then for Honeywell, she handled stock transactions. She served as the executive director for a foundation.

At the same time she was the caregiver for her mother and for her grandmother who had Alzheimer's. She describes "trying to hold it all together" and being on "overload." She says, "I was in charge of everything: everything at my job, working with a foundation, running for city council."

Overload took its toll. Two back surgeries and two knee surgeries left her unable to work but not yet able to retire. She realizes, "I had to think about me, which is so hard."

Beverly believes that she went through all she did for a reason. She says that her struggles gave her the ability to say, "You can do it." She remembers telling herself over and over during her most difficult times, "You can make it."

In spite of her health issues, Beverly had a long and successful career at Honeywell. After twenty-five years of service, she accepted an attractive retirement package. Work, however, did not stop at retirement. She entered a new stage of life as an entrepreneur. Her business ventures have included planning and selling worldwide adventures and introducing a new line of women's foundation garments. Some days she hardly has time for her favorite hobby, fishing!

In spite of her hard work, financial struggles forced Beverly to sell her home. She was behind on her mortgage payments and could see no way to catch up. House prices had plummeted, but Beverly saw no choice. "I said, 'I'm selling it. I can either sell it or lose it.' " She put her house on the market.

The prospect of selling looked bleak until, one day, a couple appeared in her yard. She had no idea who they were. "When I looked out the back window, the lady was skipping around. She looked as if she was in seventh heaven. The garden was just beautiful." The couple came inside to look. "The real estate salesman said my house was the cleanest one he had seen!" The couple decided to buy the house for their son.

They had a perfect credit rating, but the bank was set to foreclose in two weeks. They made an offer, and Beverly accepted. "The check came, and I was signing it six hours before they were going to lock up my house. We had to fax and then go to the sheriff's office to get everything done."

Beverly describes the garden she had to give up: two apple trees, one pear tree, one plum tree, rhubarb, and roses. One of her joys was being able to feed her friends with the products of her work. "I had to leave my garden. I didn't care about the house. It was just a house."

Now she feeds the neighborhood. Empty cupboards are a daily reality for many in the homes around Kwanzaa, but with Beverly's skill and care, vegetables are flourishing on a vacant lot next door to the church. Kwanzaa invites all who are hungry to pick what they need.

Good friends have graced Beverly's life, friends like Lisa. "I feel blessed. I've had three or four cars given to me. They're like clunkers, but they get me everywhere." One day when Lisa was helping Beverly in her garden, she stood up and said, "Sister Beverly, you need a car."

Beverly replied, "I know that, but I've got all these bills. I can't afford it."

"I'm going to take the car my sister-in-law has. It belongs to me, and I'm going to give it to you. It needs a radiator."

"I don't care," said Beverly. "I'll take it." One week later, Lisa died. Tears of gratitude closes the interview with Beverly. "That's why I cry all the time, not because I'm sad. I know what God can do. He patched me up!"

Questions for Reflection and Discussion

- Beverly speaks of her gratitude to God. For what are you thankful as you reflect upon your own story?
- Beverly says that God patched her up. In what ways has God patched you up?
- How have you been marked by your life experiences?
- How has Beverly carried on the biblical tradition and practice of hospitality?

For Further Exploration

- Read the story of the slave girl in Acts 16:16–19. How are the stories of the slave and Lydia different? Do you see any similarities? (Note that the slave has no name.)
- Where in our country does slavery still exist? (After a presentation on sex trafficking, a pastor said, "I thought slavery had been abolished.")
- Women have often lacked opportunities for church leadership. In what ways have women influenced our churches in spite of obstacles to leadership?
- Do you believe that women and men have equal opportunities for leadership in your church or denomination? Give reasons for your answer.
- Which groups in the church are underrepresented in leadership?

Part III

It is our wish that you, our readers, are discovering yourselves in the continuing story of God's faithful people. If you hunger for knowledge, if you have confronted life-changing choices, or if you have known great loss, you may find that one of the following stories is your story. It is our prayer that you will find in the ancient story and in your own story God's love, presence, and justice.

—Bebe Baldwin and Alika Galloway

CHAPTER 16

Living the Hunger for Knowledge: Eve
Genesis 2:15–3:24

T he gates of Paradise are closed. We can never again live in Eden. I wanted knowledge, but I have discovered that knowledge has a price. Would it have been better to live forever in the innocence of Eden?

You have heard my story. No doubt you have been told that I was the one who brought sin and death into the world. But let me tell you my story for it is only mine to tell.

Our Creator put Adam and me into a perfect garden. In our small world we knew nothing of pain, of backbreaking work, of diseases, or of death. We never knew hunger, because the branches of every tree and shrub hung low with fruit. The clusters of grapes were so heavy that when I gathered them, I had to cradle them in my arms. Scarlet pomegranates glistened with the sweet juice their cracked skins could not contain. The garden was like a banquet prepared and spread out for us by our generous host.

We lacked nothing — nothing except knowledge. We knew nothing of good and evil, for our Creator had denied us the fruit of one tree in the garden, the tree of the knowledge of good and evil. The Lord God had warned us that on the day we ate the fruit, we would die.

But the forbidden fruit tempted me like no other fruit in the garden. At dawn it gathered the first rays of the sun to promise the coming of a new day. By midday it had exploded into brilliant splendor as if to claim its prized place among all the fruits in the garden. At sunset its brightness mellowed to a quiet glow as if to soothe the garden's creatures into sleep.

One day as I sat gazing at the forbidden fruit, the snake appeared. (You remember that I had the first conversation in the Bible, even if it was with a snake!) The creature asked if God had really forbidden us to eat any of the fruit in the garden. When I repeated what the Lord God had said, the snake argued that we would not die. Instead, he declared that we would be like God, knowing good and evil.

Questions leapt to my mind. Perhaps they were the questions that had lurked there all along: "Why did God give us eyes to see, fingers to touch, and noses to enjoy the fragrance of the garden and then deny us its most beautiful fruit?" "Why did our Creator give us freedom to make choices and then take away our freedom?" (By the way, if you are wondering where Adam was during the conversation, let me tell you. He was sitting nearby, close enough to overhear, but not bothering to say a word. That didn't keep him from blaming me after we both ate the fruit.)

The forbidden fruit lured me. My fingers ached to hold it, to caress its warmth. I longed to squeeze the juice that was about to burst from its ripe flesh and let its sweetness drip onto my tongue. I yearned to share it with the man I was just getting to know. I was sure that sharing that prize would be like sharing life itself.

My trembling hand reached out toward the fruit and the words, "You shall not eat," sounded like drumbeats in my head. Timidly, my shaking fingers dared to touch the fruit. Immediately, it fell into my hand, as if waiting to spill its sweetness.

I broke open the fruit and called Adam. He hesitated not one moment. We shared the fruit, and it was like honey in our mouths. We felt carried away on waves of ecstasy. For the first time, Adam and I knew each other as man and woman. We embraced with joy.

But suddenly we saw something else. It was as if our eyes had been opened. For the first time we saw each other's nakedness, and we were ashamed. We raced through the garden, tore fig leaves from branches, and sewed them together to cover our bodies.

That evening we heard God walking in the garden, and we hid. When God called, we were terrified. The Creator who had walked and talked with us became our sovereign judge.

So now we are shut out of Eden. Our naïve innocence has died, and we shall never again look through childlike eyes at a perfect world. Now we know the real world where there is beauty and goodness, but also willful ignorance, heartbreak, hatred, and war. Our eyes are open now to the suffering of the poor and the oppressed.

But with our knowledge we are also finding wisdom. We are learning that good and evil are often mixed, and therefore the joy we know is more precious. We know that our knowledge will never be complete, that it will always be limited. We know that even with our incomplete knowledge, we have the responsibility to care for the world and for its people.

What is most amazing is that we are not alone outside the garden. Our Creator saw our need and clothed us. God who walked and talked with us inside the garden is the same god who is with us outside the garden.

Would it have been better to live forever in the innocence of Eden? Surely it would have been easier. Pain is a price we pay for knowledge — pain that is our own and that belongs to others. I can never go back to Eden, and I do not wish to go back because God is with us, even outside Eden. This knowledge is the beginning of wisdom. Thanks be to God!

CHAPTER 17

Living Conviction: Rahab
Joshua 2:1–21

I sell my body so I can eat. If this bothers you, tell me how else I can survive. I have a father and brothers, but no one protects or supports me.

My house is in the city wall. That should tell you something about my place in Jericho society. I don't move in the best circles. I go to the town well to draw water at midday when everyone else has deserted the city streets. My town tolerates me because people say my trade is necessary, but they still scorn me. Men come to me in the dark cloak of night, shielded from prying eyes by my house in the wall, or so they think. There are no secrets in Jericho. So they come — patriarchs and young men, soldiers and merchants, tillers of the soil and those who have never dirtied their smooth, callous-free hands. I provide the service they demand. My job is to make weak men feel strong and old men feel young again. I drive away their worries, at least for a few moments of ecstasy.

But lately, when I welcome the men to my door, even the proud and brave men of Jericho, they gaze back at me through the eyes of frightened little boys. They confide stories too terrifying to tell in the streets: reports of a hoard called Israelites, landless tribes who outwitted their Egyptian slave-masters. They were delivered by a powerful god whose name is too holy to speak. Everywhere they go, their bravest enemies are slaughtered, and only dust and rubble mark the places where cities once stood. "It is only a matter of time," they whisper, "before those fierce warriors attack us."

Last evening, as daylight was just beginning to fade, I was starting my preparations for the night. I was perfuming myself when a knocking, soft but urgent, interrupted me. I was annoyed; I needed more time. I hesitated, but the knocking grew louder. When I could ignore it no longer, I opened the door a crack. Without looking at me, two men pushed past into the room. Catlike, they moved through my small quarters, alert eyes taking in every detail until they found what they were looking for, the ladder that led to the roof. Without hesitating, they climbed nimbly to the rooftop.

Fear seized me, then certainty. The men were Israelites — spies! Overhead, I heard their footsteps. They were surveying our defenses, measuring out death to my city. I knew that I must sound the alarm, alert the guards. But my body refused to move; I felt paralyzed. I told myself that as soon as they left, I would run and alert the city.

After what seemed like a very long time, they came downstairs. "We'll stay here tonight," said one. I nodded and pointed to the rooftop.

The night crept by slowly. I barely closed my eyes, and I opened the door to no one. The confusion and terror in my heart felt like wild beasts tearing at me. The spies had not harmed me, but would they kill me to make sure I did not alert the guards? Could I sneak out and sound the alarm while the spies slept? I was gripped by pangs of fear when I realized that the Israelites might already be surrounding us, covered by darkness but awaiting some signal from the spies on my roof. I wanted to weep for my mother and father and for my brothers and sisters. I held their lives in my hands.

Loud pounding at my door broke the troubled sleep that finally came to me at dawn. A commanding voice shouted, "Open up! Enemy spies! Bring them out! We know they're here!"

At that instant I made my choice. Our puny gods could not protect us from the Israelites' god. I called out, "Wait! I cannot receive you now. I'll be quick." I hoped they did not hear the quavering in my voice.

I flew up the steps to my roof. The spies were already awake and reaching for their weapons. I signaled them to lie down. I threw stalks of flax over them and checked to make sure their cover was complete.

The pounding grew louder and the voices more demanding. I feared the men would break down my door. In my haste to get down, I slipped and fell the last three steps. Pain stabbed my ankle as I rushed to the door. As soon as I unbolted the door, it flew open and I fell back.

Horrified, I recognized the men as aides to the king himself. For an instant my will wavered. Could I, a powerless woman, defy the lord of Jericho?

The soldiers saw at once that no one was hiding in my room. The leader pointed to the steps. One of the men began to climb.

Trying to keep my voice from shaking, I bowed before the leader and said, "My lord, listen to me. Two men came to me. I had no idea who they were. They left before the city gates would close. If you hurry, you'll catch them."

The soldiers looked at the leader for directions. The one on the steps paused. The leader pointed to the door. His urgency allowed no more time for searching. When they left, my heart was pounding so hard I feared it would burst. Another moment of delay and I don't think I could have covered up my deceit.

As soon as they left, I bargained with the spies — my life and the lives of my family in return for theirs. I told them to hide in the hills for three days until the king called off the search. Then I used a rope to let them down to the ground through a window in my house. When the Israelites attack the city, a scarlet rope in my window will mark my house, and my family and I will be spared.

It is morning now. The king trusts no one. I know he has posted guards around my house in case I lied about the spies.

So I wait. I pray that the Israelites will come soon. I pray that the God who freed the slaves will care about a poor woman who uses the only skills she has so she can eat. I, too, want to be free. Then I can join the Israelite women when they dance and sing praise to God. Their God will be my God!

CHAPTER 18

Living Pain and Praise: Hannah
1 Samuel 1:1–2:10

My heart soars when I sing and dance with the women of Israel. My voice rings loud and clear above all the others when we sing

There is no Holy One
like the Lord, no one besides you;
there is no Rock like our God.

1 Samuel 2:2

When we whirl and step to the beat of our timbrels, no one can resist the rhythm. The children bounce with joy, and the old clap their hands. But there is no song in my heart today.

How can I sing to a god who is taking my son — the child I carried in my womb and nursed at my breast? I am carrying him now, holding him tight so that I can breathe in his sweet breath. His dark thick curls are catching my tears.

Before my son was conceived, I made a solemn vow. The time has come when I must keep my vow. We are on our way to Shiloh where I will surrender my child to Eli, the priest.

I made my vow at the harvest festival. As we do every year, the family — my husband, Elkanah; his other wife, Peninnah; and her children and I — had gone to the festival. There Elkanah and the other men offered the sacrifices the priests tell us we must bring to the Lord.

While the men were gone, we women prepared the cakes for the feasting that began when Elkanah returned with the family's share of the burnt offerings. And what a feast it was, for everyone but me!

It was Elkanah's duty to divide the meat. He gave generous servings to Peninnah, who had given him sons and daughters. To me, his barren wife, he gave only a small portion. I was too upset to eat even that.

Puzzled, Elkanah asked why I was not eating. I tried to tell him how painful it is to be childless. He answered, "Hannah, don't be sad. Am I not more to you than ten sons?" How little he understood!

166

Did he think he could make up for Peninnah's taunting as her belly swelled again and again? Did he think his words could take away the shame when other women waggled their fingers at me and whispered, "Barren! Cursed!"? Did he think he could make up for the tears I shed each month when my bleeding came again? No, he did not understand. (Besides, he already has heirs, the sons of Peninnah. His heritage is safe.)

I had done everything the wisewomen told me to do. The midwives sang their songs and gave me remedies. In my desperation, I even baked cakes and offered them to the queen of heaven — secretly, of course. I could not risk the wrath of the priests who command us to sacrifice only to Israel's God. But what do the priests know of women's pains? Every month the bleeding comes again.

I clung to the stories I had heard so many times — the stories of the mothers of Israel. I loved the story of Sarah. When Abraham invited three strangers to rest from the heat of the desert, the Lord visited them. Sarah and Abraham prepared a generous meal, and as they ate, the Lord promised a son to the barren Sarah. How joyfully I would have prepared a feast for such a promise. Then there were Rebecca and Rachel, both barren until the Lord remembered them and gave them children. I often wanted to scream, "Why doesn't the Lord remember me?"

That day at the feast, I knew what I must do. I waited until the feasting ended, until the men were in their tents, dull with meat and drunk with wine. The air was still heavy with the smoke of many burnt offerings when I set out, hurrying to the temple. I had made up my mind to throw myself on the mercy of the God of our mothers.

When I arrived at the temple, Eli the priest was sitting at the door. His eyes were heavy; I think he scarcely noticed me. If he saw me at all, he probably wondered, without much interest, what a woman was doing alone in the sanctuary.

So I poured myself out to the Lord. I let go all the grief, all the disappointment, all the anger. "Why?" my heart cried, "Why did God single me out? Why did the Lord refuse to grant me children?" My rage and sorrow took hold of me. My whole body shook.

Suddenly I realized that I was not alone. I looked up and saw Eli standing tall above me. His face was blotched with purple and the veins in his neck bulged. "Woman, you are drunk!"

Stunned, I told him that I was not drunk but that I had been begging the Lord to show me mercy. His face softened a bit, and he shrugged. He left me alone, saying that he hoped the Lord of Israel would hear me.

So I made my vow. I promised that if God would take away my curse and give me a son, I would give him back to the Lord. (All our firstborn belong to God, of course, but we redeem them with silver.) I promised that there would be no redemption for my son. He will serve the Lord all the days of his life.

So my son was born, the child of my vow, the son given me by the Lord. I named him Samuel, which means "I have asked him of the Lord." According to our sacred law, my husband could nullify my vow, but he did not. So now that Samuel is weaned, I must give him back. I will keep my vow.

But God is faithful and hears the cries of the brokenhearted. God will remember me, and I will praise him.

> *My heart exults in the Lord;*
> *my strength is exalted in my God.*

1 Samuel 2:1

CHAPTER 19

Living Wonder: Mary
Luke 4:14–30

J esus is my son, but I have asked myself over and over, "Who is this son of mine? His name means 'savior,' but can he save himself?" Not knowing is a heavy weight crushing my heart.

Everyone here in Nazareth has heard about the amazing works Jesus has been doing in Capernaum. So when the news spread that he was on his way home, everyone — the hopeful, the curious, the skeptics — rushed out to meet him. The crowd followed him everywhere, waiting and watching to see him either prove his power or show himself to be an imposter.

I'll admit that I was both anxious and hopeful. "Perhaps," I thought, "if Jesus does something truly wonderful, my neighbors will stop whispering about me, calling me the mother of a madman." I thought that maybe, then, the weight would lift from my heart.

Today on the sabbath, the whole village followed Jesus to the synagogue. The noisy crowd hushed as he stood to read from the sacred scroll. Even as he began to read, however, heads were shaking, and I knew that some of my neighbors were thinking, "He is only the son of Joseph, the carpenter. How can he know more than the rest of us?"

Jesus read from the prophet Isaiah: the promise that God's servant brings good news to the poor and freedom for the oppressed. Suddenly I knew that the words of the prophet were for us. We are the poor; we are the oppressed!

Barely turning my head, I lifted my eyes to see how my neighbors were taking in the words. I saw tears glistening on the cheeks of some, a shadow of hope on other faces. Behind me a wrinkled crone whispered to a squirming grandchild, "Maybe the Lord will at last show mercy." I wondered if I dared to be proud of my son.

But Jesus must have seen something else in the crowd. "No doubt you are thinking," he said, 'Physician, heal yourself.' You want to see what the people in Capernaum saw. No prophet is accepted in his own country!"

His words rang out like a trumpet. With that call all the suspicions in the crowd began to harden into hostility. I wanted to scream at Jesus, "Stop! Stop! We want to hear good news!"

But Jesus went right on, telling stories from our scriptures. He told the story of the prophet Elijah, who fed a foreign widow when the Israelites were starving. He told the story of the prophet Elisha's healing of a leper, not one of the many lepers in Israel, but another foreigner!

No wonder tempers flared. We are the people God chose! We try to keep our sacred law, but the Romans feast while our children cry from hunger. We are losing our lands, our ancient heritage, so pagans can build palaces. Our backs are breaking from the taxes we pay. We want good news, not stories of what God has done for pagans.

I struggled to breathe. I could feel the stirring in the crowd. A shout, "Kill him!" pierced the sabbath's quiet.

The crowd turned into a mob. It surrounded Jesus and drove him forward to the cliff outside the village. All the fear, the pain, the anger against our occupiers came to life like a beast aroused from sleep, ready to strike. I heard a woman scream. Someone shoved me, and I recognized the sound of my own voice. I didn't know whether to throw myself at the feet of the village elders and plead for my son's life or to run for my own.

Nearly frozen by fear, I followed the mob. As I did, scenes from my life and my son's life passed before me. I saw a terrified young woman, barely more than a girl. I was promised to a good man, but I was pregnant. Would anyone believe my story? I fled to my cousin Elizabeth. She called me "blessed."

I saw myself delivering my son in a stable in Bethlehem, far from the comfort of my mother. I saw Joseph and myself fleeing with our child in the middle of the night. Later, we heard of King Herod's massacre of the children.

I saw the three of us in the temple in Jerusalem. Heartsick and desperate, Joseph and I had searched for Jesus for three days. Finally, we went to the temple to pray for the safe return of our son. There we found him, talking with the rabbis. Both outraged and relieved, I scolded, "Why have you treated us like this?"

But Jesus answered, "Don't you know that I must be in my Father's house?"

Yes, I think I knew then what I have always known in my heart. My son listens to another voice. I have never been able to forget the chilling words the old man Simeon spoke to me when Joseph and I took our infant son to the temple: "A sword will pierce your own soul too."

Suddenly, there was silence ... absolute silence. I looked up, hardly able to see through the tears that clouded my eyes. The crowd parted. Jesus was walking through the mob. He was looking off into the distance, as if he was being called by a voice no one else could hear. His attackers watched in stunned silence.

Today I saw a new kind of power in Jesus, not the power the Romans hold over us, but a power not of this world.

But I have so many questions. "Why Jesus? Why my son?" Perhaps my biggest question is, "Why, of all the Jewish women, did God choose me to be the mother of this man?"

CHAPTER 20

Living Sisterhood
Matthew 2:13–18

This story is dedicated to the mothers who have lost daughters and sons to violence in a world we have not made safe for children.

The terrible news attacked Bethlehem like a swarm of angry locusts. Their victims swatted and cursed but could not drive them away. At first the villagers thought the news was nothing but a foolish rumor. They pretended not to have heard. But soon the news gathered itself into a menacing shape that stalked every parent in Bethlehem and lurked like a terrifying monster in every house.

No one knew who first told the news. Whatever the source, no one — rabbi or illiterate peasant, merchant or carpenter — dared to speak aloud of what was too terrible to name. Everyone knew that King Herod was cruel, but even he would not issue so monstrous an order — or so the villagers told themselves. Surely there was no need to fear. The report could be no more than the work of a demonic trickster.

One of the mothers who deluded herself was Rachel, the wife of Thomas, the village carpenter. Rachel had delivered their first child, a son, attended in her home by her mother, sisters, and wisewomen of Bethlehem. On that same night, another woman had given birth to a son in the innkeeper's stable. That mother and her husband were strangers in Bethlehem. They, like throngs of others, had crowded the village to register to be taxed.

Like everyone in Bethlehem, Rachel and Thomas were poor, but they dreamed of a glorious future for their son. When Thomas saw his infant son swinging his tiny fists, he nearly burst with pride. "Look at that strength," he boasted. "He will be the best carpenter in all Judea." When the baby cried, Rachel heard, in the wailing of the hungry infant, the future voice of a great rabbi. But deep in the hearts of Rachel and Thomas was the hope of all Jewish parents that their son would be the promised one, the Messiah, the one God would send to liberate the Jews from the Roman occupiers.

Both the boys, Rachel's son and the child born in the stable, were two years old when the terrible news turned into reality. On that day the king's soldiers stormed into Bethlehem. It was as if the gates of hell

172

had opened to let loose an army of demons. Screams of helpless fury pierced the village as parents pled with soldiers to spare their sons. Rachel watched in horror as Thomas fought, bare fists challenging cold metal swords, to save their son. When the soldiers left, swords red with the blood of innocent children, a terrible keening rose in Bethlehem. Finally there was the silence, the silence of dreams destroyed. In Jerusalem King Herod slept soundly that night, secure that no son of Bethlehem would live to be crowned King of the Jews.

Like all devout Jews, Rachel and Thomas repeated twice daily the most sacred words of the Torah. "Hear, O Israel: The LORD is our God, the LORD alone. You shall love the LORD your God with all your heart, and with all your soul, and with all your might." (Deuteronomy 6:4–5) But secretly, lest she be accused of blasphemy, Rachel asked, "How can we love a God who shows no mercy?"

But she was fertile and, as the seasons passed, Rachel and Thomas had seven other children. Loved as they were, none filled the emptiness left by the firstborn. For many years Rachel woke in the night, wailing, hearing again her child screaming as the soldiers tore him from her arms.

Nevertheless, their children brought Rachel and Thomas great joy, along with bewilderment common to parents. When Sarah showed no interest in women's work and slipped into the carpenter's shop when she should have been helping Rachel bake bread, Rachel despaired. "How will we ever find you a husband?" But Rachel could never stay angry for long as she watched her daughter grow in beauty and wisdom. When Matthew was too sick to go to the synagogue school but disappeared to explore the hills around Bethlehem, Rachel shed tears of frustration. But who could punish too severely a son who spoke so tenderly to his mother?

Like all families they had their disagreements. From the time Joel could toddle into the carpenter's shop, he picked up scraps of wood to form play swords. Long before his voice deepened to become a man's, he announced, "The only way to be free is to kill the Romans!"

Amos, who loved sitting and talking with the rabbi, argued, "You're wrong! If every Jew will obey our sacred law for just one day, the Messiah will come. Then God will fight for us!"

Joel laughed. "That is foolish talk. We must fight for ourselves. Then maybe the Messiah will come."

So Rachel lost a second son when Joel left with only a vague explanation of where he was going. Rachel knew he was going to join the freedom fighters. She shed more tears when Amos bade the family goodbye. He announced that he was going to Galilee to seek a new rabbi who was preaching the Kingdom of God.

The seasons passed and so did the years. Another Passover was approaching. Rachel told Matthew, her oldest son, "I will go with you to Jerusalem this year for Passover. This will be my last Passover in Jerusalem." These were not idle words. Her joints ached and her vision blurred. She mourned the death of Thomas, her life's companion. Nevertheless, she was determined to travel to Jerusalem for the holy days.

The walk to Jerusalem was demanding, but Rachel's heart soared when she glimpsed, at last, the holy city. When Rachel and her family entered the city the day before Passover, her joy should have been complete. Instead, even the stones seemed to shout warnings to the pilgrims. Everywhere, soldiers watched, set at any moment to draw their swords.

Then there was the whispering, always after furtive glances to make sure no soldier could hear. "Have you seen the rabbi called Jesus?" Some reported, "We were there when he rode into Jerusalem on an ass. We shouted 'Hosanna! Save us now!' " Others, whose eyes sparkled with excitement, reported that Jesus had driven the money changers out of the temple! Others muffled laughter, awestruck at the way Jesus had debated lawyers in the temple. A few barely breathed the words, "Can he be the Messiah?" As the hours passed before the Passover Seder, the whispering grew more cautious. Dread hung over the city like black clouds before a storm.

But it was with a spirit of hope for her children and grandchildren that Rachel gathered with her family for the Passover Seder. They shared the traditional foods: the Passover lamb from the temple sacrifice, bitter herbs that recalled the Hebrews' suffering, the unleavened bread the Israelites ate when they fled Egypt. They told the freedom story and prayed that someday they too would be free. But when the next morning dawned, Rachel awoke with a sense of foreboding she could not name.

At the ninth hour the news shook the city. "Crucified! Jesus is crucified!"

Rachel felt her chest tighten. She had to fight to breathe. "Why?" she asked herself. After all, this was only one more crucifixion. Didn't crosses rise with any hint of rebellion? Why was this execution any different? Rachel tried in vain to shake her terror.

Then at noon blackness fell over the city like a pall. It was as if even the sun chose not to look down. When the earth rumbled and shook, Rachel hid her face in trembling hands. "Who was this Jesus?" Suddenly she was struck by a new thought. She remembered the day her son, Amos, had left to follow a Galilean rabbi. Was it possible — could it be that his name was Jesus?

The sabbath, meant to be the most joyous of days, followed. Rachel stayed in the inn, careful not to violate the sabbath law, but after sundown she walked to the spice market. There she would buy the spices for which she had saved a few coins. The streets that usually bustled after the sabbath calm were nearly deserted. Those who had ventured out pulled their cloaks tight around themselves and gazed into the distance as if they could make themselves invisible.

At the spice seller's stall, Rachel waited to bargain with the merchant. Before her stood three women. They too were buying spices, including nard used for burying the dead. They talked in low tones, but Rachel heard the whispered word, "Jesus." Rachel stole a quick glance at them but immediately averted her eyes.

When the three left, Rachel, who had also completed her business, felt compelled to follow them. When the women paused and, for a moment, turned back, Rachel ventured a few cautious steps toward them. Two of the women, as if alert to some threat, stepped between Rachel and the third woman. One thrust out her hand, signaling Rachel to leave them alone. Yet Rachel saw in their eyes no hostility, only fear. Rachel ignored the warning and stepped toward the one they were shielding. She was heavily robed; eyes, red with weeping, barely peered out between the folds of the veil. In those eyes Rachel saw searing pain, a reflection of her own.

Rachel said nothing as if to speak would transgress holy ground. But the other woman, as if to answer Rachel's unspoken question, clutched Rachel's hand. She murmured, "My son ... "

Her companions cast warning looks that implored, "Hush, we don't know this woman."

But the woman repeated, "My son ... "

"Where is he?" whispered Rachel.

"He died ... "

Stunned, not knowing what to say, Rachel asked, "How old was he?"

"He was born in Bethlehem thirty years ago."

Rachel stiffened. "Impossible!" she snapped. "There was a massacre. The king sent his soldiers. All the babies were killed."

"My husband had a dream. We fled in the night."

Rachel felt her heart turn to ice. She hissed, "Then my son died that yours might live."

There was a long silence. Finally the woman spoke. "Perhaps it will be said someday that my son died that others may live."

The two women embraced, and their embrace was a prayer that went straight to the heart of God. It was the prayer of women everywhere that someday no mother's son or daughter will die in the cause of injustice, oppression, or greed.

Author's note: Matthew 2:18 refers to Jeremiah 31:15. There were many "Rachels" after the massacre in Bethlehem.

Selected Resources

Ackerman, Susan. *Warrior, Dancer, Seductress, Queen: Women in Judges and Biblical Israel.* The Anchor Bible Reference Library. New York: Doubleday, 1998.

Bach, Alice, ed. *Women in the Hebrew Bible.* New York: Routledge, 1999.

Black, Kathy. *A Healing Homiletic: Preaching and Disability.* Nashville: Abingdon Press, 1996.

Cannon, Katie Geneva; Isasi-Diaz, Ada Maria; Pui-lan, Kwok; Russel, Letty M., eds. *Inheriting Our Mother's Gardens: Feminist Theology in Third World Perspective.* Philadelphia: Westminster, 1988.

Cone, James H. *The Cross and the Lynching Tree.* Maryknoll, New York: Orbus Books, 2011.

Craddock, Fred B. *Luke. Interpretation: A Bible Commentary for Teaching and Preaching.* Louisville: John Knox Press, 1990.

Crossan, John Dominic; Reed, Jonathan L. *Excavating Jesus: Beneath the Stones, Behind the Texts.* San Francisco: HarperSanFrancisco, 2001.

Darr, Katheryn Pfisterer. *Far More Precious than Jewels: Perspectives on Biblical Women.* Louisville: Westminster/John Knox Press, 1991.

Fischer, Kathleen. *Women at the Well: Feminist Perspectives on Spiritual Direction.* New York/Mahwah: Paulist Press, 1998.

Gaventa, Beverly Roberts; Rigby, Cynthia L., eds. *Blessed One: Protestant Perspective on Mary.* Louisville: Westminster John Knox, 2002.

Goldstein, Elyse, ed. *The Women's Torah Commentary.* Woodstock, Vt.: Jewish Lights Publishing, 2000.

Grant, Jacquelyn. *White Women's Christ and Black Women's Jesus: Feminist Christology and Womanist Response.* American Academy of Religion Series. Atlanta: Scholars Press, 1989.

Hare, Douglas R. A. *Matthew. Interpretation: A Bible Commentary for Teaching and Preaching.* Louisville: John Knox, 1993.

Haskins, Susan. *Mary Magdalene: Myth and Metaphor.* Old Saybrook, Conn.: Konecky and Konecky, 1993.

Hayes, Diana. *Hagar's Daughters: Womanist Ways of Being in the World.* 1995 Madeleva Lecture in Spirituality, Saint Mary's College, Notre Dame, Ind. New York/Mahwah: Paulist Press, 1995.

Hearon, Holly E. *The Mary Magdalene Tradition: Witness and Counter-Witness in Early Christian Communities.* Collegeville, Minn.: Liturgical Press, 2004.

Leloup, Jean-Yves, trans. and Row, Joseph, trans. *The Gospel of Mary Magdalene.* Rochester, Vt.: Inner Traditions, 2002.

Meyers. Carol. *Discovering Eve: Ancient Israelite Women in Context.* New York: Oxford University Press, 1988.

Newsom, Carol A.; Ringe, Sharon H., eds. *The Women's Bible Commentary.* Louisville: Westminster/John Knox, 1992.

Olson, Dennis T. *Numbers. Interpretation: A Bible Commentary for Teaching and Preaching.* Louisville: John Knox. 1996.

Plaut, W. Gunther, ed. *The Torah: A Modern Commentary.* New York: Union of Modern Hebrew Congregations, 1981.

Rohrbaugh, Richard L. *The New Testament in Cross Cultural Perspectives.* Eugene, Ore.: Cascade Books, 2007.

Saso, Sandy Eisenberg. *But God Remembered: Stories of Women from Creation to the Promised Land.* Woodstock, Vt.: Jewish Lights Publishing, 1995.

Skloot, Rebecca. *The Immortal Life of Henrietta Lacks.* New York: Crown Publishers, 2010.

Sloyan, Gerand S. *John. Interpretation: A Bible Commentary for Teaching and Preaching.* Atlanta: John Knox. 1988.

Weems, Renita J. *Just a Sister Away: A Womanist Vision of Women's Relationships in the Bible.* San Diego: Luramedia, 1996.

Williamson, Lamar Jr. *Mark. Interpretation: A Bible Commentary for Teaching and Preaching.* Atlanta: John Knox Press, 1983.

About the Author

The Reverend Bebe Baldwin is a retired Presbyterian minister and an advocate for social justice. She received her Master of Divinity at United Theological Seminary of the Twin Cities, with honors in systematic theology.

Baldwin's relationship with Kwanzaa began with her service on the presbytery committee that assisted in organizing the church. She now serves on a presbytery task force that works with Kwanzaa in interpreting Kwanzaa's unique mission.

She is an active member of the Presbyterian Health, Education, and Welfare Association (PHEWA). In 2004 Presbyterians for Disabilities Concerns, a network of PHEWA, gave her the Nancy Jennings Award for advocating with and for people with disabilities. She is legally blind. In 2011 PHEWA honored her and her husband, Rolland, with the Rodney T. Martin Award for outstanding service in the movement for social justice.

In *Living Water, Living Stories,* her skills in biblical interpretation, her ability to listen and inspire trust in interviewees, and her love of storytelling come together with her passion for social justice.

About the Editor

The Reverend Dr. Alika Galloway is a womanist theologian, a community activist, and a pastor. She and her husband, the Reverend Dr. Ralph Galloway, serve Kwanzaa Community Presbyterian Church in Minneapolis. The church is internationally known as a model congregation specializing in interactive community engagement. She is executive director of Northside Women's Space, a safe place where girls and women who have been exploited by trafficking and the sex trade can find support and healing.

Dr. Galloway received her Master of Divinity in womanist theology and world religions from Johnson C. Smith Seminary and her Doctor of Ministry from Virginia Union Seminary. She serves as an adjunct professor in womanist ethics at United Theological Seminary of the Twin Cities.

She serves on the Board of the Minnesota Council of Churches and is a member of Minneapolis's Urban Health Network. At the 2010 General Assembly of the PC (U.S.A.), Kwanzaa was honored for outstanding justice work in gender equality and HIV/AIDS and for addressing issues related to the urban poor and the disenfranchised. In 2011 the Women's Press of Minnesota honored her with the Changemakers Award and the National Council of Churches inducted her into the Circle of Names.

36413324R00119

Made in the USA
Charleston, SC
02 December 2014